...as many as touched (Jesus) were made perfectly whole.

Matthew 14:36, KJV

With contributions from:

LISA HARPER
AMANDA MAGGARD
TRICIA SMITH-EDRIS
PAM TUCKER
STACEY TOL
STEPHANIE LIND
JEAN THOMASON
JEAN BOONSTRA
OMAYRA MANSFIELD
CARLA GOBER PARK
ALICIA PATTERSON
TAMI CINQUEMANI
ROBYN EDGERTON
ADRIANA PASOS
And many others

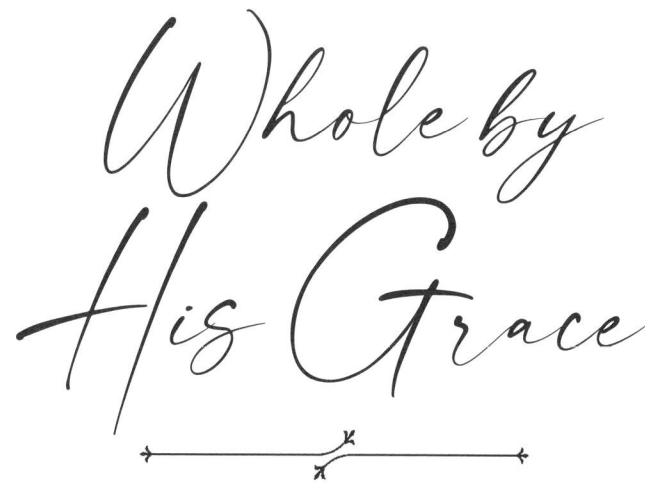

3 - MINUTE DEVOTIONALS
FOR WOMEN

AdventHealth Press

AdventHealth

WHOLE BY HIS GRACE
Copyright © 2012, 2021 AdventHealth Press
Published by AdventHealth Press
605 Montgomery Road, Altamonte Springs, Florida 32714

EXTENDING *the* HEALING MINISTRY *of* CHRIST

Editor-in-Chief:	Todd Chobotar
Managing Editor:	Denise Rougeux-Putt
Promotion:	Caryn McCleskey
Production:	Lillian Boyd
Copy Editor:	Pamela Nordberg
	Jaclyn Mallan-King
Cover Design:	John Lucas
Interior Design:	Kimberly Sagmiller

PUBLISHER'S NOTE: This book is not intended to replace a one-on-one relationship with a qualified health care professional, but as a sharing of knowledge and information from the research and experience of the author. You are advised and encouraged to consult with your health care professional in all matters relating to your health and the health of your family. The publisher and author disclaim any liability arising directly or indirectly from the use of this book.

Not to be reproduced. No portion of this book may be reproduced, stored in a retrieval system, or transmitted in any form or by any means – electronic, mechanical, photocopy, recording, or any other – except for brief quotations in printed reviews, without the prior written permission ofthe publisher. All rights reserved.

The Scripture versions cited in this book are identified on page 266, which hereby becomes a part of this copyright page.

Portions of this book were previously published in
CREATION Health Devotional for Women

For special orders, events, or other information, please contact:
AdventHealthPress.com | 407-200-8224

AdventHealth Press is a wholly owned entity of AdventHealth.
Library of Congress Control Number: 2020924813
Printed in the United States of America
ISBN: 978-0-9963692-8-2 (Print)
ISBN: 978-0-9963692-9-9 (EBook)

For more Whole Person Health resources visit:
AdventHealthPress.com
CREATIONLife.com

Contents

Welcome 9

A Deeper Joy 10
CARLA GOBER PARK

If You Can't Find Joy in Your Day, Create It! 13
OMAYRA MANSFIELD

Life in the Arena 17
TRICIA SMITH EDRIS

Boyfriend Points 21
JEAN BOONSTRA

Friendships 25
AMANDA MAGGARD

It's All About the View 29
STACEY TOL

Out of the Torrent 32
ALICIA PATTERSON

Broken to Brand-New 36
PAM TUCKER

A Warranty of Grace 40
TAMI CINQUEMANI

Lazarus the Cat 43
LISA HARPER

Daniel's Leadership Principles 47
ROBYN EDGERTON

God's Provision 52
TRACEY MASTRAPA

Come and Go 55
SPERANTZA ADRIANA PASOS

Forgiven 58
JULIE COOK

The Healing Yet to Come 61
JACLYN KING

The Healing Power of Joy 65
STACEY TOL

Secret Pain and Hidden Scars 68
DELORES FRANCOIS

The Gift 72
MARY KENDALL

Love Heals 76
DOROTHY BROWN

Consider the Lilies 79
LAURA BRADFORD

This Race Is Not Just for The Runners 82
MULENGA MUNDENDE

Seven Years of Bad...Seven Years of Plenty 86
CYNTHIA MERCER

Waiting for Morning 89
ALICIA BRUXVOORT

Pushing Through Life 93
STEPHANIE LIND

The Master Gardener 96
DIANE THURBER

The View from 26 Weeks 100
JAMIE SANTA CRUZ

A Worthy Resolution 104
HELEN HEAVIRLAND

The Gift of Choice 108
DELORES FRANCOIS

Somersaults in the Sky 112
TERRI CRUZ

Never More Than You Can Handle 115
SHARON JALLAD

Perfectly Planned 118
LIZBETH FERNANDEZ

Forgiving Daddy, Healing Me 121
BETTY KOSSICK

That Newspaper on the Floor! 125
ANA BOUDET FORMAN

Sweet Words 129
PATTY KNITTEL

Hearing by God's Grace 132
KIMBERLEY QUINNIE

I Love You Just the Way You Are! 136
DAWN S. BROWN

A Turnaround 140
ARLENE SALIBA

God Says, "I Love You" 143
JOANNE CORTES

Heaven's Stand-In 146
COLLENE KELLY

Trust the Expert 150
CARLA BAKER

Too Busy to Rest 153
CHERYL MOSELEY

My Friend's Baditude 156
CODI JAHN

Fear Not the Cat 159
JEAN THOMASON ("MISS PATTY CAKE")

Just a Routine Test 162
PATRICIA BODI

Angels All Around Us! 165
JUDITH NEWTON

Taking the Plunge 168
ALICIA BRUXVOORT

Really Lord, Her? 172
CODI JAHN

I Got You, Girl! 175
DOROTHY DAVIS

Act As If 178
SARA ALSUP

Are You Afraid? 182
JOANNE CORTES

Craft Night 185
JENNI GLASS

The Gift of Trust 188
EVE RUSK

Because He Paid for Me 192
CARMALITA GREEN

Confessions of a Culinary Klutz 195
JAMIE SANTA CRUZ

Follow the Plan! 199
DELORES FRANCOIS

The Tender Trust of Life 203
COLLENE KELLY

Life Is Amazing Live It Well 206
LINDA NORDYKE HAMBLETON

The Magic of Believing 209
LORRAINE JAMES-STIGGERS

On Eagles' Wings 213
FRANCES MORFORD

For Melinda 217
GLADYS JOY! BAZEMORE

Safe as a Deer 221
LISA CLOUZET

Infusion 224
ARLENE SALIBA

A Girl's Wish, A Woman's Existence 227
SHAMETA WEBB

Trust 230
CHERYL MOSELEY

Exposed 234
NONI BETH GIBBS

The Wiggly One 237
JANET SCHLUNT

Wake Up! 240
ASHLEY TARDIF

Gardening 101 243
PATRICIA BODI

Waiting for God 247
LYLAN SHEPHERD FITZGERALD

Walk On 251
LAURA BRADFORD

Bonded by Wounds 254
MONICA AMES

One of My Favorite Gifts 257
LISA CLOUZET

About the Authors 261
About the Publisher 268
Resources 270

Welcome

…as many as touched (Jesus) were made perfectly whole.
Matthew 14:35, KJV

The Scriptures tell us that when Jesus was here on this Earth, everyone who touched him was made completely whole. Such is the power of Jesus to heal and transform lives. We all need that touch. This world and its troubles can leave us bruised and bleeding. Where is Jesus so we can touch him and be healed? Although he is not physically with us now, we can still touch him. As we spend time in his creation, he speaks softly to our hearts. As we interact with those who love us, we see his gentle face in their look and tone. As we read his Word, his voice lovingly speaks to us. And he speaks to us through the stories of others—stories of struggle and sadness, hard lessons learned, but also joys and triumphs and victory. As you read these stories by women just like you, may you be strengthened and encouraged to face each day with joy, knowing you are touching Jesus, and by his touch he is making you whole.

Denise Putt
Managing Editor

A Deeper Joy

CARLA GOBER PARK

> *"The Lord is close to those whose hearts have been broken.
> He saves those whose spirits have been crushed."*
>
> **Psalm 34:18-19, NIRV**

Grief is powerful. It helps us cry when we need to cry and work through pain that is often complex. It comes and goes like waves of the ocean and stops us in our tracks like the sudden realization that we are lost or have made a wrong turn. Like a sad song, it can make us remember, even when we had not thought about remembering.

Grief is difficult, powerful, healing, scary. Sometimes people say the right thing. At other times, there is no right thing to say. Grief is not two roads that diverged in a yellow wood. It is one road that doesn't diverge at all, but winds its way through sadness, joy, ups and downs as though it were its own captain of a ship or conductor of a train. We are the riders, noses pressed to the window to catch a glimpse of a familiar landscape, only to find ourselves viewing something altogether new.

Then suddenly, yes suddenly, we notice the yellow flower pushing its way through the rocks, announcing its resurrection from death, or what seemed to be death. This is life–blooming amidst the impossible, bringing joy on the side of a cliff where unseen audiences clap and cheer.

The journey of grief is never over, but at some point, we begin to believe that life really does move forward and that the new landscape begins to bring hope.

And through it all, the most loving of Hands holds ours–with Eternal Nose pressed to the window with us, helping us know beyond the shadow of a doubt that a second Heartbeat echoes ours, in time with what we feel and in tune with whatever song we choose to sing at the moment.

I have felt grief. I know that my grief is unlike yours, but one thing is similar. When we cry, an Eternal Heart causes the rain to drench the earth, and when we sigh, an Eternal Breeze becomes a wind that roars through the trees. How do I know? Because I've seen it. What I feel, God feels more deeply. *"Who has gathered the wind in his fists? Who has wrapped the waters in his garment? Who has established all the ends of the earth? What is his name or his son's name? Surely you know!"*

(Proverbs 30:4, NASB). *"He causes his wind to blow and the waters to flow"* (Psalm 147:18, NASB). *"The Lord is near to the brokenhearted and saves those who are crushed in spirit"* (Psalm 34:18, NASB).

If You Can't Find Joy in Your Day, Create It!

OMAYRA MANSFIELD

> *"This is the day that the Lord has made; we will rejoice and be glad in it."*
>
> **Psalm 118:24, NKJV**

We all have ups and downs in our lives, both personally and professionally. This is simply the nature of who we are as human beings. Practicing emergency medicine and working in the healthcare space can be challenging, as a typical workday may be affected by a devastating loss. There are days where you question God, his will, and his existence. Days when you make a new cancer diagnosis in a patient or have to break the news of a family member's death. I have experienced those days where coming back to work the next day seems impossible, the heartbreak and pain we see unendurable. It can be easy to overly focus on these moments. But we risk missing the beauty and joy that coexist: the pregnancy that was confirmed to be healthy, the patient suffering a heart attack who will recover after being rushed to the catheterization lab, the parents of a sick child reassured that he will feel better soon.

How we proceed when faced with challenges and adversity depends on the choice in attitude and mindset that we make, and the outlook we choose to have. It doesn't take working in the extreme environment of an emergency department to experience these highs and lows, ups and downs. For every thunderstorm, after the intense wind and heavy rain have passed, oftentimes if we step outside and look towards the light of the sun, we can see the rainbow. It takes the intentionality of looking for that light to pull us out of darkness. How we manage our actions and emotions during these turbulent times not only impacts and determines the outcome, it ultimately leaves a lasting impression on us and those around us, particularly those we love.

Finding gratitude in each day with intentionality is a practice I have developed in my life and made an integral part of my routine. It has helped to level out those days that are difficult and to reframe my focus. The simple act of relishing and recalling the joyful things in each day, no matter how large or small, can have a dramatic impact on your perspective.

Begin each morning with a moment of gratitude. Before getting out of bed, take a deep breath and think of one specific thing you are grateful for, and as you do, imagine a weight that comes off your shoulders, feeling the levity in the moment.

At night as you prepare for bed, reflect on your day. Consider three specific moments or thoughts that fill you with gratitude. Feel the peacefulness that comes with each thought.

I reflect on the Psalm to remind myself that each day is one that the Lord has specifically created with us in mind. He created the day with love for us in his heart. Even when it appears that we are wandering, lost in a grey cloud, feeling helpless, there is a plan for us. And no matter how lost we may feel, we are where God wants us to be. There is joy to be found if we look around with intentionality, and we should seek to rejoice in it. And if the joy cannot clearly be seen, own the process and set about creating it yourself!

Creating joy may sound difficult to do, but sometimes joy can be found in the smallest things. I had a particularly difficult day at work one day and, as I drove home, I felt despair. I realized in that moment that I had an opportunity to reframe my own perspective and fight this sense of despair with joy. I decided to surprise my children and jump into the pool at our home as soon as I arrived, still wearing my work clothes. The smiles on my children's faces and the sound of their laughter in the air still stays with me. This simple act to help myself overcome despair resulted in a gesture of love that my children truly enjoyed.

Don't ever be afraid to bring joy into your own life and the lives of the ones you love! "Rejoice and be glad in it!"

Life in the Arena

TRICIA SMITH EDRIS

*"Let me give you a new command. Love one another.
In the same way I loved you, you love one another."*

John 13:34, MSG

You may be familiar with the following passage from Theodore Roosevelt's famous "The Man in the Arena" speech (slightly edited):

> *It is not the critic who counts; not the woman who points out how the strong woman stumbles, or where the doer of deeds could have done them better. The credit belongs to the woman who is actually in the arena, whose face is marred by dust and sweat and blood; who strives valiantly; who errs, who comes short again and again, because there is no effort without error and shortcoming; but who does actually strive to do the deeds; who knows great enthusiasms, the great devotions; who spends herself in a worthy cause; who at best knows in the end the triumph of high*

achievement, and who at worst, if she fails, at least fails while daring greatly . . .

I don't know about your experience, but mine has included time in the arena. I have been marred in dust and sweat and blood. Repeatedly erring and coming up short time and time again. Striving valiantly and not so valiantly for my devotions and achievements.

Regrettably, if I am honest, I have also spent time as the critic. Pointing to where others have stumbled, or where the doers could and should have done better.

There are even times when I have been both the critic and the one fighting in the arena—at the very same time. The inner voice pointing out my own imperfections, missteps, and failures.

If you have ever spent time in the arena, you know it is not an easy place. However, despite its hardships and struggles, its beauty lies in the fact that it is where we find all the action. And along with the lows are the triumphs and the victories. All mixed together. I believe the arena is where followers of Jesus are called to live and work and play.

I have worked at AdventHealth pretty much my whole life. It was my first job, and I suspect in a few more decades, it could be my last. While there are many reasons why I love AdventHealth, the biggest one by far is the people who work here and their willingness every day to run into the arena and fight for healing, for health, for wholeness.

When the novel COVID-19 virus emerged, I saw doctors, nurses, respiratory and laboratory technicians, environmental services team members, front desk clerks, and cafeteria staff run into the arena every day, for months. I saw administrative, finance, supply chain, human resources, and facilities leaders all run into the arena with support and critical resources. Day after day, month after month. Knowing both successes and failures, the people of AdventHealth continued to strive and dare greatly.

Why? What compels someone to live in the arena? Is it devotion? A call to duty? I believe it is love.

Writer and commentator Peggy Noonan describes the power of love this way in an article in *The Wall Street Journal*:

> *The way I see it, courage comes from love. There's a big unseen current of love that hums through the world, and some plug into it more than others, more deeply and surely, and they get more power from it. And it fills them with courage. It makes everything possible.*

The "big unseen current" from my worldview is the God of Love.

Paul, in Ephesians 5, explains it this way:

Mostly what God does is love you. Keep company with him and learn a life of love. Observe how Christ loved us. His love was not cautious but extravagant. He didn't love in order to get something from us but to give everything of himself. Love like that (Ephesians 5:2, MSG).

Love moves us out of comfort and safety into the arena, and love is the sustaining force that keeps us going back in day after day.

My prayer is that every day we connect with and experience the powerful loving God, and that this love empowers and energizes us to love each other.

Boyfriend Points

JEAN BOONSTRA

"Be still, and know that I am God…"
Psalm 46:10, NIV

So, here's what we'll have to do on your graduation weekend," I said emphatically, my fingers poised, ready to indicate the number of tasks to be accomplished.

My adult daughter tensed visibly. "Mom," she protested, "I graduate from college *next* May."

I noticed her crinkled forehead but pressed on. "If you two want to get married at the end of the summer, we'll have to get that all done over your graduation weekend," I concluded.

My oldest child seemed to think about her words before speaking. "Mom, he hasn't even proposed yet," she finally exhaled.

I glanced down at my hands—my fingers still extended to indicate the tasks I'd just insisted had to be accomplished a year from now. Tasks for a wedding that was still just a dream. I clasped my hands together to release the tension—in my hands and in the air.

"I just want to enjoy him being my boyfriend," she added with the magnanimity of a much older woman.

I wish that this interaction with my daughter was an isolated incident. Instead, it was part of a pattern that—until recently—dominated my life. By nature, I am a planner and a to-do list-maker. I welcomed Monday mornings with gusto and fidgeted and felt grumpy on unscheduled Sunday afternoons. Like most of us during the 2020 stay-at-home orders due to the coronavirus, I initially canceled plans and cleared my calendar. I woke up the first Sunday to an unscheduled afternoon that turned into dozens of unscheduled mornings and afternoons to follow.

The prospect of an empty calendar frightened me, and I set to work on a plan. I had a new Bible and I devised a plan to read and mark it. The first morning sitting at my kitchen table this verse seemed to be written just for me: *"And on the seventh day God finished his work that he had done, and he rested . . ."* (Genesis 2:2, ESV). God rested from his work of creation. This verse and concept weren't new to me. I weekly kept a day of rest—at least in theory. In that quiet moment at my kitchen table, I saw this rest as a sweet gift of love.

In the unscheduled days that followed, I wrestled with accepting this gift. One evening, I left the house to walk around the neighborhood—I didn't make a call to a colleague, or listen to the news or an audio book. I walked without earbuds and listened to the birds, the wind, and the traffic. I felt my shoulder muscles loosen. I walked again the next evening, and the one after that—a new pattern. In the morning, I doodled in the margin of my journal, losing track of time as I penciled flowers, birds, and branches.

When the day of rest arrived, I stepped outside and sat in the sunshine. Free from the list of duties that normally consumed this day, I struggled to rest my thoughts and my mind. I persisted, and each week my mind quieted a little more easily. God reminded me that he created a living being—someone he wants to share love and a relationship with. He didn't create an automaton designed to check off a task list. He created this world, and then he rested. He wasn't tired. He rested so that I would give myself permission to rest and draw closer to him.

"Mom, there's the doorbell," my daughter called out to me. "Are you expecting someone?"

"No," I answered, getting up from my desk and walking to the door. Opening it, I spotted a brown paper bag with my daughter's name on it. Smiling, I called out, "It's for you!" Still in her PJs, my girl lifted up the bag and gasped happily. "I didn't think he'd really order this for me," she gushed, lifting out her favorite blended drink. "He just earned some serious boyfriend points," I teased, then stepped away so that she could call the gift-giver.

Sitting back down at my desk, I remembered the conversation I'd had with her a few days ago. I realized I was wrong–then and now. This sweet gift didn't earn him boyfriend points. Love doesn't keep track of points or demerits. Life and love are about enjoying being.

Friendships

AMANDA MAGGARD

> *"Just as iron sharpens iron, a person sharpens the character of her friend."*
>
> **Proverbs 27:17, CJB (with small edit)**

I've known her since the sixth grade.

Together, we went to school for nearly ten years, worked at summer camp, watched movies and gossiped at sleepovers, sat next to each other in band, traveled on school trips, and were college roommates. She was there when I met my husband nearly eighteen years ago, and she was my maid of honor when we said, "I do." I was there when she met her husband working at summer camp, and I was her maid of honor when they married five years later.

Since college graduation twelve years ago, we've each crafted a very different life journey. Aubrey and Josh spent several years living in South Korea, teaching English as a second language and traveling all over the world. About seven years ago they moved back to Lincoln, Nebraska, and launched a photography business. In contrast, Michael and I moved to Orlando after college to be close to family and to work in healthcare administration, and we've been here ever since. (That's right; I'm the boring friend)

Aubrey and I live very different lives today, and we've had unique experiences since we graduated college. In fact, I can probably count on one hand the number of times I've seen her in the past decade. But no matter what changes may have occurred since our last visit–changes in jobs, countries visited, or even the number of people in our household–when we see each other, it's like no time has passed.

I was talking with a colleague last week about friendship–about the kind of friend you see after weeks, months, or years apart, and it feels like no time has passed. That is the kind of friendship I share with Aubrey and a number of other very special folks in my life. These are the friends who ground us as human beings; they remind us who we are, where we've come from, and where our lives are going.

I think these friends can also help us learn more about our relationship with God, or the type of relationship that he longs to have with us. In Exodus 33:11, the Bible describes the friendship between God and Moses. It says: *"So the Lord spoke to Moses face to face, as a man speaks to his friend"* (Exodus 33:11, NKJV).

Can you imagine being able to sit and talk with God face to face? To grab frozen yogurt and catch up after a long day? Or meet up for Sunday morning breakfast and a walk? This intimacy is what God hopes to have with each of us, just as he had with Moses. The type of friendship where we can open our heart and share with him our joys, our fears, and the minutia of our day.

God designed us to share this type of closeness with other human beings, too. Friends bring us comfort, laughter, a shoulder to cry on, and an ear to listen. Proverbs 27:17 says, *"As iron sharpens iron, so a friend sharpens a friend"* (NLT). In other words, healthy friendships can make us better people.

In my ten-plus years at my workplace, I can definitely say that some of my best friends are those I've met through work. (Maybe I need to get out more . . . just kidding!) I am incredibly grateful for these friendships and how they've both supported and shaped my character over the years.

If you have a chance today, maybe you can reach out to the quiet person on your team and ask if they want to grab coffee. Or chat with God on your drive home about the highs and lows of your day. Or take a minute to tell one of your friends how much they've meant to you in your journey.

On that note, I think I'm going to text Aubrey . . .

It's All About the View

STACEY TOL

*"The heavens declare the glory of God;
the skies proclaim the work of his hands."*

Psalm 19:1, NIV

When I was sixteen, my dad accepted a job offer that would require our family to move from the evergreen mountains of Southern Oregon to the high desert landscape of Eastern Oregon. The ranch-style home we'd lived in for seven years, with its mountaintop vista and five wooded acres, sold at a tidy profit. I was excited to begin looking at houses with my parents, knowing we could afford to "level up" with our new place.

By the end of two days, the local realtor was able to show us every house in our price range for sale in the small town. There were A-frames, Colonials, and even a dome house. All of them had more square footage than the home we were leaving behind. My favorite was a white one that was the biggest—and most expensive—of all, but really, I would have been fine with most of them.

Our last stop was seven miles out of town. As the realtor pulled into the graveled driveway, I looked with incredulity. *Why had she driven us to this place?* It was a dump! There was a gigantic steel garage, and a number of outbuildings including a dirty chicken coop. The "house" itself was a well-worn doublewide trailer. It couldn't even compare with our last home, let alone all the potential houses we'd been looking at. Feeling tired and completely disinterested, I didn't bother to get out of the car. Surely my parents would dismiss this flytrap in a matter of moments. When five minutes turned into fifteen, I was surprised. When fifteen dragged into forty-five, I was truly puzzled. But when my parents finally returned to the car and announced that they were going to buy the property, I was completely flummoxed.

I didn't see what they saw. I noticed windows with bent screens, but they were looking at what lay beyond the windows. They saw a seven-acre sloping field of grass and wildflowers. They saw a view of the land and sky that stretched broadly in every direction, only meeting at the hazy horizon where the earth begins to curve. They were not buying a doublewide. They were buying sunrises, sunsets, and front row seats to the nightly appearance of the Milky Way.

Though I had to help hose out the chicken coop and kill a startling number of houseflies, I became utterly spoiled by the view. The magentas and purples of God's sunset palette were breathtaking, and the sheer number of stars in the nighttime sky was unfathomable.

Now, like most Americans, I live in a light-polluted urban area where only the brightest of stars and constellations can be seen. The sunrise is blocked by trees and houses, the sunset by offices and overpasses. While there is plenty of good to be said of my home, sometimes I just need more sky in order to breathe.

When the stress of a busy schedule or the length of a "to do" list makes me feel like hyperventilating, going to the park, where I can see a bigger chunk of sky, resets me. It makes me remember how small my current worries are in the scheme of things.

When I am able to truly get away to a place humankind hasn't illuminated, I lay beneath the night heavens and stare with wonder at the trillions of stars that blur at the fuzzy edges of our galaxy. The greatness and beauty of God's creation put my life and daily concerns back into perspective. I am re-centered and renewed. Able to breathe again. It's really all about the view.

Out of the Torrent

ALICIA PATTERSON

*"Let the morning bring me word of your unfailing love,
for I have put my trust in you. Show me the way I should go,
for to you I entrust my life."*

Psalm 143:8, NIV

My husband and I are on a break: Two weeks in Colorado! It is the first time we've had this much time together without the children for twenty-three years. True story. There is a waterfall outside my window as I write. The ceaseless motion and rushing sound of the white water pouring over the rocks has brought me peace over the last few days. But today, I imagine what it would be like to be one of those rocks in the middle—with the weight of the water pouring, rushing, pounding down. Because that is what my life has felt like for so long, and it's hard to catch my breath.

The device in my hand is the channel, and from it pour emails, texts, and shopping opportunities.

Commercials, articles, and unasked-for videos pop up and try to grab my attention, even on Bible sites and alongside praise music on YouTube. Anxiety-producing news items pop up unbidden. The work/home balance has broken as I can be accessed anywhere and feel responsible to respond. I've been drowning in the world's torrent.

I have looked at the emblem on my phone and laptop for years and wondered about that small apple with the bite out of it. Does it represent the world's last deception, so similar to the one Eve held in her hand? You can be like God! Through this device you hold, you can be all-knowing and omnipresent! And in knowing and being present, all-powerful!

Yet meanwhile, our souls are drowning in the deluge of things that demand our attention. Our relationships are more shallow, and our thoughts as well. Our peace is diminishing, and anxiety grows.

I have been doing something that helps me. It slows my heart rate and the speed of my thoughts. It reminds me Who God is and that he is still in control. And that is memorizing Scripture. I read it every morning too, and journal, and that is its own kind of helpful. But the difference between casual Scripture reading and memorizing is the difference between smelling good food, or licking it and chewing, and swallowing food. Then you digest it, and it becomes a part of you.

I love memorizing the Psalms because David is real. He cries out to God about how he feels. He describes in detail how unfair or dark things seem. But then, David reminds himself how God has worked in the past. Present fears encroach again, but he tells himself the stories of God's past goodness and future promises. Eventually, he is able to praise God and trust him again as God becomes more real than the current torrent of events.

I know what you're thinking, "I'm not any good at memorizing. She must have a remarkable mind." Nope. It's hard for me too. I have chemo brain from a year-long bout with cancer, post-menopausal mind, and the difficulty concentrating the e-age has brought. It's not easy. It's not fast. But it's worth it.

I have heard that, while it can bounce quickly back and forth, the mind cannot think about more than one thing at once. Memorizing slows my mind, and anxious thoughts depart while I fight to concentrate. Slowly the world recedes and with relief I enter into the ancient and very present story of the God who would rather die than be without us. I come out hope-filled and stronger.

Right now, I am memorizing Matthew 27:24-54. I want to have what Jesus did for me digested and made a part of me so that no one and no circumstance can take it away. I cannot tell you what a blessing it has been—and in so many ways. I have learned from the temptations Jesus endured on the cross and have been enlightened by many parallels with other parts of the Bible. I am more secure in his love.

Memorizing this passage helps me remember how much Jesus loves us because of how much he went through for us. His determination. His bravery. His love. It helps me know God will never leave us or forsake us—no matter what it looks like. It was so dark in every way when Jesus was dying. But the greatest victory ever was taking place.

I am inviting you to try this too—for the first time, or again. If you would like to do this with the encouragement of friends, check out https://lifestreams.org/irecite/. Put your phone down. Start with something small, like Psalm 143:8, the Scripture above. And watch while God starts to bring you out of the torrent and helps you order your life again.

Prayer: *Help, Lord! Everything is so insistent, and Your voice seems more and more distant. Teach us how to find our footing, get out of the falls, and get some perspective. Help us breathe and remember how much bigger You are. How are You speaking to us today? What are You saying?*

Broken to Brand-New

PAM TUCKER

> *"For I know the plans I have for you"* declares the LORD, *"plans to prosper you and not to harm you, plans to give you hope and a future."*
>
> **Jeremiah 29:11, NIV**

If you haven't experienced brokenness yourself, then you know someone who has. Painful experiences, relationships, career pitfalls, divorce, financial loss, and even death are just a few examples of brokenness. When life throws roadblocks of pain in your direction, all you have are storm clouds and rain with very little sunshine.

Perhaps it was an unexpected pregnancy that derailed your plans for college and a career. Maybe you had a dysfunctional relationship that reshaped you emotionally; now, you always feel insecure. Maybe you unwittingly went from one abusive relationship to another because that's all you knew. As you look at your reflection, all you see are scars. You are also aware of the invisible scars that others can't see. You wince, remembering the pain that caused them.

It is easy to fall into despair and justify curling up into a ball to avoid the gut punches that life throws daily. The really hard part, especially for those of us who have been wounded, is to maintain hope. We've hoped before and were disappointed. We've hoped for love and were taken advantage of. We've hoped for peace and married someone who screamed every time we did something wrong, even when it was right. We've carried our burdens so far and for so long that our bodies and minds are bent under the weight. It is too much to bear alone, yet it's easy to withdraw socially. We are in the valley of despair more than we are on the mountaintop of victory.

Sometimes I just kept praying for God to stop the pain and make it go away. The more I reached out to God, the more the storm increased in intensity. And it was all I could do to just stay in the boat and not give up and jump overboard in despair. It was hard to even imagine how I would make it through each day. I pretended that everything was okay, even when it wasn't. I wanted others to feel comfortable; like most people, they didn't know what to say to someone in the middle of a storm.

Weeks can become years and you feel as if life is just passing you by. Yet for some unknown reason, you still hold on and hope. I can't explain it, but I know it because I lived it for a really long time.

It was in those darkest times that I caught glimpses of Jesus. That is when my hope took root. With every trial, I gained more strength as I drew closer to him. It was down in the deepest valleys that I met him face to face.

Whatever valley you are in now, he knows what you need, and he will carry the burden for you. We can be assured that he will not allow the experiences we have had to destroy us. He promises there is nothing we have lost that he won't replace, and he will help us start over again. He offers healing waters for our troubled, wounded souls. He will hold us in the shelter of his arms so that we can carry on and have the life he intends for us.

This may be a new experience for you as you grow in relationship with him. It may even be your first loving relationship that isn't manipulative. His love is pure, and he knows that you need to trust in order to love. I can promise you, he won't fail you.

For others, he promises to do it again when we fail. He will recreate us in his image; he will cleanse and make us whole again. We may think we have fallen too far from him, and that we are unworthy of his love, but his grace is far greater than anything we may have done.

We may have to start all over again, and life may take us on a new journey. It might be a new home, country, job, or even a new relationship or marriage. Whatever your circumstances, he will be with you.

Allow the seed of hope to be planted in your heart right now. He will not allow your life to stay broken no matter how terrifying the situation you are currently in. He will repair the broken pieces into a brand-new creation.

A Warranty of Grace

TAMI CINQUEMANI

"God saved you by his grace when you believed. And you can't take credit for this; it is a gift from God."

Ephesians 2:8, NLT

I tend to be a bit of a clean freak. I am cheered by organized closets. The smell of Pine-Sol takes me to my happy place. And I find something lifegiving about vacuum lines. (Okay, maybe "clean freak" is too harmless a term for my disorder.)

We recently replaced all the windows in our house. After thirty-two years, it was time. Not only was it a wise decision for energy efficiency, the new windows were made in a way that made cleaning them easier from both inside and outside. This is very important when it comes time for the annual fall cleaning of my windows. Did I mention I have a disorder?

When the job was accomplished, the workmen were very careful about leaving all the windows sparkling clean. I was delighted! However, about an hour after they left, I noticed a spot on my kitchen window. Upon closer inspection, there were actually several spots. Nothing large—all about the size of a pin head, but still. I immediately grabbed the Windex.

First, I worked from the inside. No luck. No worries; I simply brought my cleaning rag outside. Still no luck. I think I must have gone from the inside to the outside of the window three times, furiously trying to remove the spot. No matter how hard I wiped or what cleaning solution I used, nothing I did made a difference.

I have discovered this principle of life—that when I want to do what is right, I inevitably do what is wrong. I love God's law with all my heart. But there is another power within me that is at war with my mind. This power makes me a slave to the sin that is still within me. Oh, what a miserable person I am! Who will free me from this life that is dominated by sin and death? Thank God! The answer is in Jesus Christ our Lord. So you see how it is: In my mind I really want to obey God's law, but because of my sinful nature I am a slave to sin (Romans 7:21-25, NLT).

As is true for every descendant of Eve and Adam, I am a broken human, scarred by sin, and lost in my depravity. So, does that make me naturally fall to my knees in surrender, realizing I have no way of making myself clean? No sir! I pick up my bottle of outward goodness along with my rag of self-righteousness, and I go to work! I put some effort into the inside by eating a vegetarian diet, drinking the required amount of water, maybe even attempting the occasional raw food detox cleanse. Then I get started on the outside: faithful church attendance, posting inspiring Scriptures on social media, maybe delivering groceries to my elderly neighbors. Though all of these things may be worthwhile and beneficial to my life, they're completely worthless as an attempt to cleanse my soul and remove the guilt of humanity's sin. My "spots" aren't going anywhere if this is my plan for removing them.

God saved you by his grace when you believed. And you can't take credit for this; it is a gift from God. Salvation is not a reward for the good things we have done, so none of us can boast about it. For we are God's masterpiece. He has created us anew in Christ Jesus, so we can do the good things he planned for us long ago (Ephesians 2:8-10, NLT).

We called the manufacturer and explained our dilemma. With no questions asked, the window was replaced. I now look out my kitchen window and view my front yard through a clear pane.

My own efforts are worthless and will only lead to discouragement and emptiness. Thankfully, I can trust that my Creator (my Manufacturer) knows my dilemma and has always had a plan for my redemption. Through undeserved and unmerited mercy, when God looks at me, I am crystal clear, cleaned by the saving grace of Jesus.

Lazarus the Cat

LISA HARPER

"How can we possibly thank God enough for all the happiness you have brought us?"

1 Thessalonians 3:9, CEV

One bright summer day, a tiny orange tabby appeared on the rock wall outside my bedroom and smiled. Although I tried to shoo that baby cat away, he stubbornly refused to leave my yard.

To make matters much worse, a few days after my uninvited feline guest's arrival, I woke up at the crack of dawn to the sound of dogs barking. I stumbled to the window and rapped sharply on the glass, which usually causes my Jack Russell terriers to be quiet. Only this time their barking became louder and more frenzied. I muttered and grumbled as I climbed out of bed and wriggled into a sweatshirt.

I opened the back door groggily and yelled, "Harley and Dottie, hush!" hoping my disheveled appearance would be enough to silence them and I wouldn't actually have to leave the comfort of the kitchen and traipse up the dewy hill for a face-to-snout reprimand. Then I noticed Dottie had something in her mouth and was furiously shaking it. I sprinted toward her yelling, "Dottie, no!" because even from a distance I recognized her new chew toy as the homeless kitty.

By the time I got there, Dottie had placed the slobbery ball of orange fur on the ground and was looking at me with the same shamefaced expression she wears when she's destroyed yet another dog bed. After shouting, "Bad, bad dog!" I scooped up the limp, barely breathing kitten and carried him into the house, thinking, *Every living thing deserves to have somebody with it when it dies,* and assuming I'd be burying the poor little thing within the hour.

Miraculously, that plucky kitten recovered, so I christened him "Lazarus." Within a week he was climbing trees and stalking butterflies and harassing me for fresh tuna. I couldn't help but spoil him, since I felt responsible for his near-death experience. More than once I found myself walking through the cat paraphernalia aisle at Target sheepishly piling things into my cart!

Lazarus even wormed his way into Harley's and Dottie's hearts and took to cuddling with them on chilly nights, purring away contently.

Sometimes, when I watched him frolicking with them in the field behind my house, I was tempted to call out, "Lazarus," you idiot, those are the same mutts who tried to kill you!" But instead, I would just grin and think, *That silly cat has captivated us all.*

Almost a year from the day I met him, Lazarus wasn't at the back door waiting for his breakfast as usual, and I was immediately concerned. It wasn't like Lazarus to miss a meal. For the next several days, I went on long walks calling his name and even put up a "Lost Cat" sign in Puckett's, our local mom-and-pop grocery store.

About a week after Lazarus disappeared, a woman called because she had noticed the sign and recognized Lazarus as the cat she had seen run over by the car in front of her when she was driving her kids to school. She carefully explained that he hadn't suffered, because he'd been killed instantly. I told her that I really appreciated her call and was glad to know definitively what had happened to him. Then I hung up the phone, sat down heavily on my bed, and cried.

I still miss Lazarus. When he died, it was almost as if I had lost my pinky toe—not something you tend to appreciate, yet its absence leaves you noticeably off balance. I find myself often glancing up at the crook in the tree where he used to lounge and feel my heart skip a beat when I see another tabby that resembles him. Grieving for that cheeky critter has been a poignant reminder for me to be more appreciative of and attentive to all the little "kisses from God" that are woven into our lives.

This story is adapted from a chapter in *Stumbling Into Grace*, by Lisa Harper (Nashville: Thomas Nelson, 2011). This excerpt has been reprinted with permission from Thomas Nelson, Inc.

Daniel's Leadership Principles

ROBYN EDGERTON

"So then, my dear friends, stand firm and steady. Keep busy always in your work for the Lord, since you know that nothing you do in the Lord's service is ever useless."

1 Corinthians 15:58, GNT

I have a younger brother, Doug, who made my childhood fun. He was always up for an adventure! And with him there was often a "dare" in the equation, a moment to prove myself. I'd muster up the courage to run through a tunnel with puddles and worms or ride my bike out of bounds, all because of Doug's dares.

There was another dare we sang about in church.

Dare to be a Daniel,
Dare to stand alone!
Dare to have a purpose firm!
Dare to make it known.

I loved singing that song because Daniel is one of my favorite Bible characters. Stories of Daniel were the best. He and his friends were kidnapped and taken to Babylon. He refused to eat the king's food. His friends were thrown into a fire but didn't burn. The most amazing story was when Daniel spent the whole night sitting in a cave with hungry lions.

But Daniel also teaches us lessons I never thought about as a kid. Daniel was an amazing leader. He modeled leadership values that apply to us today as we serve and work with others. As I think about Daniel's leadership, I find these principles he modeled.

Principle #1: Know Yourself

Daniel was one of three governors King Darius had put in charge of his kingdom. The king often singled Daniel out for one-on-one conversations, and the other governors suspected he was going to be promoted over them—which he eventually was.

Being jealous, they plotted. Appealing to the king's ego, they tricked him into signing a law stating that only King Darius was to be honored. Anyone found worshipping someone other than the king would be put to death.

King's law or not, Daniel knew what he would do. Years before, he had chosen what he believed and how he would live. When temptations arose, he didn't have to stop and think about his course of action; his *choice* had already been determined.

***Know Yourself** — Decide **who** you are and **how** you will live.*

Principle #2: Be Consistent

The other governors knew Daniel well, too. They knew that he lived by his convictions and prayed regularly. Although Daniel was aware of the penalty for worshipping God, he still knelt by his open window and prayed. Just as he always did. Just as his enemies predicted.

***Be Consistent** — Your behavior and decisions should be predictable.*

Principle #3: Have Your Team's and Leader's Backs

In one's work, reporting structures often change, along with new bosses and new priorities. Daniel had similar challenges. He served as a leader for five kings in Babylon. Three are mentioned in the Bible.

Nebuchadnezzar–the king who captured Daniel and his friends

Belshazzar–the king until the Medes and Persians sacked the country

Darius–the king who conquered and took over Babylon

Those were the days when kings would not just oust leaders from past governments; they killed them, their wives, and their children, too. Yet Daniel not only *survived* five regimes, he was also respected and honored in each.

It's because each king knew Daniel could be trusted. Daniel had his leader's back. In fact, when Daniel was honored for interpreting King Nebuchadnezzar's dream and the king offered him the number two position in his kingdom, Daniel said, *Don't forget about my friends; honor them, too.*

Have Your Team's and Your Leader's Backs — Like Daniel, be trustworthy.

Principle #4: Speak the Truth

Daniel was often called to the palace to have the hard conversations. While others lied to the king, Daniel told the truth.

He told Nebuchadnezzar that because he was not following God, his kingdom would be taken away for seven years and he would live in the field like an animal–not good news to have to share.

Yet Daniel spoke the truth. He told King Belshazzar he was about to lose his kingdom to the Medes and Persians because he had disrespected God. Some would have lost their head for saying something so bold. But the kings didn't hate Daniel for being truthful because they trusted his motives–which gave him the platform for speaking honestly.

Speak the Truth — *When your team knows you have their back, you can speak honestly.*

Today, I continue to think of Daniel, and trust God to help me follow Daniel's leadership lessons both in my personal and professional life.

God's Provision

TRACEY MASTRAPA

"Then the Lord's word came to Elijah: Go from here and turn east. Hide by the Cherith Brook that faces the Jordan River. You can drink from the brook. I have also ordered the ravens to provide for you."

1 Kings 17:2-4, CEB

Several years ago, my husband made a drastic career change. This was a prayerful journey for us because in so doing, he would not only be starting from scratch after twenty years of establishing credibility and building experience, but we would also be considerably cutting our family income. We recognized the ramification of this change, but a desire for new learning and reclaiming a sense of joy were worth the financial sacrifice. We walked fully into this journey with courage and faith that God would provide.

Just a few short months after settling into our planned life change, the unexpected happened. I lost my primary source of income due to changes in supply and demand. Half of the earnings I had relied on for ten years dissolved due to restructuring.

We adapted our lifestyle and refocused our attentions. Our prayers were for wisdom and sustenance.

I can recall many instances of God's provision during that time of lean, though one particular answer to prayer always stands out in my mind.

It was a Sunday, and I was planning our weekly menu in preparation for shopping the next day. I vividly remember the conversation with God about my desire for fresh produce. In my planning, I knew exactly how much money I had spent on fruits and vegetables in the past. My prayer sounded something like this: *God, I've got a few frozen fruits and vegetables that I can work with this week. You know my desire. I ask that if You see fit, You will provide the money for fresh produce this week.*

Monday morning dawned, and I prepared to get out early to do my shopping. Before setting out, I checked my inbox and found that I had received a message from an intermittent business partner asking me to fill a small consulting role. The compensation for the work to be done was the exact amount I had planned for the food budget that week, including the added costs for the desired fresh produce.

While this small miracle is basic and almost childlike in nature and focus, it was one in a series of answered prayers that God used to speak to our family during that time. He was reminding us of his sustaining power and giving us reassurance of his plans for our earthly and eternal futures. Like Elijah at the Brook Cherith, God sent us physical sustenance that only he could provide. Through his simple acts, he showed his mighty power to control life's circumstances. God is alive and active in the nuances of our lives. He has shown me through the stories in Scripture, like those of his provision for Elijah, that he is real and involved. Through my own experiences, he continues to provide evidence that he is working on our behalf today just as he worked for his people in the past. It gives me hope and strengthens my faith for today and what is yet to come. God cares about the details of our lives, and I know that I can trust in his provision.

Come and Go

SPERANTZA ADRIANA PASOS

"…And be sure of this: I am with you always, even to the end of the age."

Matthew 8:20, NLT

Come and go—two words that seem to describe my life lately. I'm either *coming* from someplace or frenetically *going* to the next on my ever-changing schedule. Sometimes it feels like I'm on a merry-go-round, wanting to get off but afraid to try for fear of falling flat on my face. Have you ever felt that way?

Jesus also came and went—a lot—while he walked on this earth. His days were filled with activity as he healed the sick, ministered to the poor, fed the hungry, had mercy on the tired, encouraged the weary, and blessed the multitudes.

Because he knew how hectic our lives would be, he left us his method of success—a secret formula to empower us through even the most difficult times.

Jesus' Invitation

Jesus says to you, *"Come to Me, all you who are weary and heavily burdened, and I will give you rest . . . and learn from Me, for I am gentle and humble in heart, and you will find rest for your souls"* (Matthew 11:28). Part of Jesus's secret formula is in this verse, but there is even more.

<u>Secret #1</u>–*Come to Me:* "You must come to the source of your strength–I am your strength. *'Without Me, you can do nothing.'* And I mean nothing."

<u>Secret #2</u>–*Rest in Me:* "Only when you come to *Me* will you be refreshed, renewed, reenergized, empowered. Trust *Me*, you need that oasis, because you cannot run this race on your own. I invite you to come to *Me* today and every day, because you need *My* rest–more than you know. Remember, My child, *'the spirit is willing, but the flesh is weak.'*"

<u>Secret #3</u>–*Go in Me:* "Only as you *come* to Me and *rest* in Me will you be empowered to *go* in My power. My child, I know what you are facing. I know your fears, your battles, your pain, your struggles, your triumphs, and your successes. I know everything about you. I also know that you cannot go in your own power; that's why I promise you Mine. *All authority* (all power of absolute rule) in heaven and on earth has been given to Me.

"As you *go*, know that you do not go alone. *'Fear not, for I am with you. Be not dismayed, for I am your God. I will strengthen you, yes, I will help you; I will uphold you with My righteous right hand'* (Isaiah 41:10).

"**Go** *therefore and make disciples (help the people to learn of Me, believe in Me, and obey My words)."* (Matthew 28:19).

Jesus' Assurance

"When you go, know I will go with you. I will walk beside you and encourage you just as I promised: *'For I the Lord Your God will hold your right hand, saying to you, Fear not, I will help you'* (Isaiah 41:13).

"And remember, *'I am with you always (regardless of the circumstance and on every occasion)'* (Matthew 28:18-20). So, My precious child, here is My secret formula."

Come to ME
Rest in ME
Go in MY POWER

Today–every day–*Come, Rest, and Go,* empowered by Jesus to accomplish His purpose! Will you follow his formula?

Forgiven

JULIE COOK

> *"Can a mother forget her nursing child?*
> *Can she feel no love for the child she has borne?*
> *But even if that were possible, I would not forget you!"*
>
> **Isaiah 49:15, NLT**

I got in trouble a lot as a kid. I got in fights with my sister. I refused to cooperate with reasonable requests. I once decided that I *was not* going to hike with the rest of the family even though leaving me alone as a five-year-old wasn't really an option for my parents. I mastered the temper tantrum, especially in public spaces. My parents later told me that they were reading books like James Dobson's *The Strong Willed Child* and consulting with a psychologist about how best to discipline me.

One day I had gotten into trouble . . . again. My mom was about ready to spank me when I looked up at her and started to cry. I told her, "But I try so hard to be good." My mom started to cry too; she picked me up and held me.

Have you ever felt the way I did, that despite your best efforts you still mess up? How does that make you feel? How do you believe God responds to you? Does he say, "No, you messed up one too many times! I'm not going to talk to you today." Or does he, like my mom, feel moved to compassion? Does he not, even more than my mom, want to pick you up and hold you? Two texts come to mind. The first is, *"If we confess our sins, He is faithful and just and will forgive us our sins and purify us from all unrighteousness"* (1 John 1:9, NIV). He is faithful to forgive! The second text is, *"Can a mother forget her nursing child? Can she feel no love for the child she has borne? But even if that were possible, I would not forget you!"* (Isaiah 49:15, NLT). How tender God is with us. He can't forget us, even when we mess up.

To be forgiven is one thing, but several years ago, the tables were turned, and I got to experience a similar emotion my mother felt when she picked me up. I had a student, Kari, who seemed to really enjoy getting to know me. She would often drop by my office to talk, and we would share about school and our personal lives. One day, I was grading a set of papers when I noticed that something didn't seem right with several of the students' papers. I Googled a couple of sentences from each paper and discovered that most of the papers in that assignment had been plagiarized. One of the papers was Kari's. By this time in my career, I had grown a little jaded about plagiarism and had stopped feeling angry when I discovered it. My emotional response was usually a resigned sadness. I returned Kari's paper to her, telling her that she would need to rewrite it because it was plagiarized.

Sometime later, I was at home when someone knocked on my door. Kari was standing on my front porch crying. She blurted out, "I broke our relationship!" I stood there for a moment profoundly moved; then I reached out and gave her a hug. It wasn't her conscience that she was most worried about (though I expect that played a part). It wasn't her bad grade that brought her to my door. It wasn't even her reputation that concerned her most. It was her relationship with me. That concern went straight to my heart.

I would like to think that I have it all together—that I never get angry or say the wrong thing or make the wrong choice, but that is not the case. Often, I find myself telling Jesus, "But I try so hard to be good." Often, I come to him and cry out, "But I broke our relationship!" Yet what I sense is that in those moments, he folds me into a compassionate hug; in those moments, he is moved by my sorrow. And I suspect he may even be *most* tender with me when I am saddened by a sense of broken trust. It's that safe, unbroken relationship He treasures most . . . and so do I.

The Healing Yet to Come

JACLYN KING

"Daughter. . .your faith has made you well. Go in peace."
Luke 8:48, NLT

The painful bleeding had to stop. For half of every month, I was out for the count with multiple female illnesses that were worsening in severity, compromising my health, and taking over my life.

I received the ultrasound results on my 37th birthday. Weeks later, I had a hysterectomy; suddenly, the bleeding stopped! The debilitating pain that had been my constant companion also stopped but was replaced temporarily with pain from the surgery. While this new pain was not pleasant, it didn't feel as overpowering—just a subtle reminder that the source of the hurt was removed. Now I could really heal!

Have you ever faced a situation where, literally or figuratively, the bleeding had to stop before you could make room for long-term healing? My hysterectomy reminded me of the woman in the Bible who bled for twelve years. Along with her physical symptoms were the spiritual and emotional side effects. In the Jewish culture of her time and place, her bleeding disorder made her unclean. She was considered an outcast, quarantined from her community, alone. It took an incredible leap of faith to reach out to Jesus, she being deemed untouchable. But with that connection, the bleeding stopped—*immediately*. Was that the end of her healing process, or the beginning of a more complex and complete restoration to wholeness?

After being a prisoner to her illness for twelve years, what were her next steps? Thinking about my own healing process, I can attest that it will hurt after the source of the pain is removed, but these are growing pains! Whether your bleeding is literal or figurative, you feel too sick to do much of anything else until it stops. Once it does, you may need to undergo a period of rest and recovery. Then, you have work to do! There is still healing yet to come.

Using timeless wisdom from our Bible story (Luke 8:43-48, NLT), I'd like to offer advice to anyone going through a healing process following a long period of suffering:

Step #1: Reach Out to Jesus

Notice that before the woman made a choice to personally connect with Jesus, "she could find no cure" for her constant bleeding and suffering. Jesus was and still is the cure! Like this woman, sometimes it is not until we are at our weakest point that we finally reach out to Jesus. I say the sooner the better! he is waiting for us to befriend him, but we must truly want his friendship and healing. Connecting with him is the first step toward healing; miracles can and do happen as a result. Keep reaching out to him regularly for continued healing.

It is the long-term, committed relationship with Jesus that matters most and heals best!

Step #2: Be Deliberate

When Jesus felt the woman's touch, He knew it was important. He said, "Who touched Me?" Peter responded, "Master, the whole crowd is pressing up against You." Jesus replied, "Someone *deliberately* touched Me, for I felt the healing power go out of Me" (emphasis mine). Jesus differentiated between the crowd's less mindful contact and the woman's *deliberate choice.*

Remain deliberate in your ongoing healing process. Stay close to Jesus. He will guide your choices and actions even when the path feels difficult.

Step #3: Cultivate Community

In any difficult situation, it is important to know you have support. Isolation can be dangerous and make the problem bigger. The woman in our story had been isolated in her suffering. When Jesus asked who touched him, "she realized she could not stay hidden." She explained why *in front of the whole crowd*, and that she was immediately healed. Not only did Jesus stop her bleeding, her partnership with him instantly plugged her back into community and restored her social health, too.

In all stages of your healing process, share what you are going through with someone trustworthy such as a family member, friend, pastor, or counselor.

Step #4: Keep the Faith

It was her unwavering faith that made the woman well again. Even after the first stage of healing when the bleeding stops, we must keep the same faith that God will get us through the next phases as we continue our journey to wholeness. The path isn't easy, but when we choose to partner with him, we are deliberate in our healing process, and we stay connected to community, all that is left is to trust that God will do the rest. I am here to tell you that He will!

Go in peace.

The Healing Power of Joy

STACEY TOL

*"A cheerful heart is good medicine,
but a broken spirit saps a person's strength."*

Proverbs 17:22, NLT

Tears pooled in my eyes as I lay in the darkness, in pain and unable to sleep. I was all too familiar with this particular ache; it was a chronic nemesis that I'd battled for over a decade. It only bothered me five or ten percent of the time, but when it did, I was hobbled. I'd be anchored to my bed or couch, unable to participate in the bustle of my family's busy life–unable to be a dependable wife and mother.

It killed me the year I'd promised to take my twin daughters on a horseback ride for their birthday, but instead found myself prone on the couch, breaking my promise. On one road trip that *I* had organized, it was difficult to explain to friends how I was fine one day but sequestered in my hotel room, opting out of all activities, the next. Over the years, this pain of mine caused me to miss more than I wanted to.

In the grand scheme of things though, these forced timeouts had very little impact on my life. My family was always understanding, never showing disappointment in me, and happy to fill in where they could. Most of the time, I was hale and hearty, able to run, travel, clean, bake, and do whatever else needed doing. Nevertheless, a flare-up would make me feel out of control and would wreak havoc on my normally steady emotions. Panicky thoughts like, "It's not going to go away this time" and "I'll be bedridden forever" would resound in my head, spiking my anxiety. I could feel my body tensing like a white-knuckled fist. The increased pressure only served to compound my symptoms and rachet up my pain level.

Trying to distract myself that night, I reached for my iPad. I stared numbly for a moment at its yellow glow, finally clicking on a site that offered up all the latest and greatest memes and videos to be had. What I saw barely registered until random scrolling brought me to a photo of a bulldog. He was standing proudly next to a decimated Roomba and a sign that read, "My house was under attack by a $700 Roomba. I saved us." I smiled. Next, there was a picture of a shamefaced pug and a sign that read, "I eat Crayons and poop rainbows." My smile widened. "Killed Yoda, I did," read the next sign. It was hanging on the neck of an unrepentant golden Labrador, standing over a de-stuffed body of the toy Jedi master. I giggled.

Clicking on one after another of these naughty dog "confessions," I found myself diverted by the canine chaos. The more I smiled, the more my body relaxed. As my tension eased, so did my pain. It took me a bit to realize the change—to notice I'd relaxed, to recognize I felt better. When I did, I began to see that by reining in my panic and focusing on something else, I could minimize my pain. Though I couldn't stop the flare-ups, I could do a better job surviving them. I could be better at not worrying as well.

Didn't Jesus say, *Do not worry about your life, what you will eat or what you will drink; nor about your body . . . ?* A wave of assurance and peace washed over me. It wouldn't be easy in the face of pain to worry less and laugh more, but it was doable. I clicked off my tablet and settled down to sleep with the old proverb running through my head, *A cheerful heart is good medicine, but a broken spirit saps a person's strength* (Proverbs 17:22, NLT).

Secret Pain and Hidden Scars

DELORES FRANCOIS

"He healeth the broken in heart, and bindeth up their wounds."

Psalm 147:3, KJV

Early on a Sunday morning, I placed a call to a dear childhood friend. We had not consistently stayed in touch throughout the years. However, that year, things happened in her life that prompted us to be more intentional in our communications. As we chatted about different matters, the conversation moved to our childhood and all the friends and neighbors where we lived on Connor Street.

Many of my childhood memories about my friend revolve around her sense of humor. She could always make us laugh. She was funny, and the best storyteller! She could skillfully tell scary werewolf stories, and I could almost see that old werewolf tiptoeing around outside our house in the middle of the night! She loved dancing and listening to the latest Motown hits that came out during those days. Our moms and brothers were friends–our families were close.

As our conversation progressed, we started sharing details about our childhoods that neither one knew about the other. She shared how her abusive stepfather beat her and her younger brother, and the sting of betrayal because she felt her mom condoned it. She shared how her mother was an alcoholic, and how she never felt loved by her. Her mother constantly admonished her with, "What happens in this house stays in this house!" She obediently complied. As she came of age, she started looking for love in sexual relationships that left her feeling alone and empty. She became an unwed teenaged mother. She eventually found comfort in food, which led to serious health consequences and gastric bypass surgery.

As my friend shared episode after episode of the pain of her childhood, the tears silently fell down my cheeks. I was her friend and never knew the painful secrets she held. I expressed my sorrow for all those years of the physical and mental suffering she endured. I wanted to jump through the cell phone and hug her tight.

I was compelled to share with her the story of my hidden pain and hurt during my childhood that she did not know either. I was a victim of childhood sexual abuse. An elder in our church took advantage of my mother's trust, a single mother struggling to raise six children. The abuse spanned several years. I shared with her the emotional toll it took on my life and the major self-esteem and trust issues it caused. I shared the shame and embarrassment I carried with me for so many years, and how it had affected my life to the present day. I shared the bitterness I felt toward my father because he had left us, and I blamed him because he was not there to protect his family. He left us vulnerable with a mother who did the best she could, but it was not enough to protect us from a child predator. This man was a pillar of the church and of our small community. I kept the secret pain to myself. Who would believe me?

The abuse stopped when I left home and went away to college. I finally found my voice and made it stop. Oh, but the wounds it made and the invisible scars it left so deep down inside! Like my friend, I looked for love in several unhealthy relationships.

Winding down our conversation and drying the tears, I felt refreshed. I felt a close connection with my dear friend. I was honored she chose me to share the intimate details of her painful childhood. We were not the only children on Connor Street that had a less than glowing family life. We identified other people on our street that held painful secrets too. When we were suffering in those childhood years, there were others who were also going through horrific experiences. We felt alone at the time; however, we realized we were not alone in our pain.

Life has taken my friend and me down different paths, but we have not lost our care and concern for each other. Most importantly, we have not abandoned our faith in God. He has blessed us and restored to us what we thought the enemy had taken. After all the years of struggling with our self-worth, shame, and embarrassment, God gave us back that which we thought was lost forever.

What secret pain and hidden scars are you holding inside? Oh, my friend, I challenge you to turn it over to the Almighty Physician who can heal and restore all that you thought was lost to you!

The Gift

MARY KENDALL

> *"Therefore it is also contained in the Scripture, 'Behold, I lay in Zion a chief cornerstone, elect, precious, and he who believes on him will by no means be put to shame.'"*
>
> **1 Peter 2:6, NKJV**

All eyes were on me as I stood uncomfortably before a crowd of nearly 5,000 people. I was waiting to open the simply wrapped gift my new friend, Justine, was presenting to me, and the crowd was waiting for my response. I was touched by Justine's thoughtfulness and hopeful that, though I couldn't communicate my appreciation in words, my face would express my gratitude.

I was in Rwanda, Africa. My husband and I were at the conclusion of a three-week mission trip. Every day, he had preached and I had given simple health lectures—both with the help of a translator. For three weeks, we had bumped and jolted our way down rutted, dusty roads passing fields where women with babies on their backs worked tirelessly. For three weeks, we'd passed drab, grass huts where nearly naked children played in dirt "yards." For three weeks, we had met daily with this crowd of people, many of whom had walked for several hours to be there and would walk several hours home in the dark. We had seen people who earned less than $1 a month and had worn the same, tattered clothes night after night drop money into the offering basket to help those less fortunate than themselves. We had heard choirs, singing songs about Jesus and the eternal home he's preparing for his children. And night after night, we had seen the joyful faces of people giving their hearts to Jesus for the first time as they responded to the invitations. And now this was our final gathering.

Justine had been my friend since we had laid eyes on each other. She was the first to eagerly welcome me with a hug and a smile. I looked for her every night, and every night she was waiting for me. Since we couldn't communicate due to the language barrier, we smiled a lot. Sometimes she led me through the crowd, introducing me to her family and friends. I showed her pictures of my family. Sometimes we sat together and listened to the choirs. Justine sang along, and when I recognized the tune, I sang with her. Although we spoke different languages and lived in vastly different worlds, we shared a special bond.

And now standing here listening as she spoke to the crowd and to me, I thought about how much I would miss her and her easy smile and warm hug. I thought about the "house" she would go home to and my house back in America. I thought about her tattered clothes and the clothes I was wearing–different clothes every day, purchased especially for this trip. I thought about the simple meals that she ate and the endless variety of food I enjoyed at home. I wished so badly to be able to share some of these things with her–things that would undoubtedly make her life easier, I thought. Yet in the face of her striking poverty, I could see peace and contentment in Justine's eyes. I thought about my struggle for contentment amidst bounty.

Justine handed me her gift. "Just something so you'll remember her," the translator said. I opened the gift and found a hand-woven banner inside. It was made from dried banana leaves and had black letters painted on it. I didn't know what it said, but I was touched that she had thought of me, that she had made something for me. I thanked her and smiled and assured her that I would not forget her. I wished I had a gift for her. I wished I didn't have to leave her behind–with so little.

We said tearful goodbyes and promised that we would meet again–if not on this earth then in the home Jesus is preparing. As my husband and I made our way toward our car and our final journey down the rutted, African roads, Justine came close and pressed a scrap of paper into my hand. It was just a few words: her simple, living testimony, the handwritten translation of the banner she had given me.

Tears spilled down my cheeks as I read, "To the one who has him, Jesus is everything."

Love Heals

DOROTHY BROWN

> *"But I say unto you, Love your enemies, bless them that curse you, do good to them that hate you, and pray for them which despitefully use you and persecute you..."*
>
> **Matthew 5:44 KJV**

*E*ach day as I entered the nursing unit I would see him standing at the end of the "V" in the hallway, his bright blue eyes sparkling as he managed a weak smile. His eyes were the bluest I'd ever seen. It seemed one could drown in that pool of blue, but for all their sparkle his eyes were filled with a deep sadness. He was in his mid-seventies, so I suspected he had experienced a lot of sadness in his life. He always had a large Bible in his possession and would cry whenever we talked. It was a busy, locked mental health unit and I'd only read the pertinent information in his chart. He had been admitted for depression. The oral report received at the beginning of the shift didn't give much information either, except that he remained quiet and depressed. Even for a man in his seventies he was handsome, and it seemed those beautiful blue eyes could swallow you whole. One son was in the Air Force and visited often. He had another son, younger, who was in prison. I felt sure that must be part of the reason for his sadness.

Being of African American heritage it was not unusual to experience prejudice from some of the patients in my care, even from the mentally ill, so it was welcome relief to care for someone who appeared to appreciate me. I was not on duty when he was initially admitted, so I missed the historical report. He received me without prejudice, so I didn't mind that the charge nurse daily assigned me to be his nurse.

One day as I tried to get him to open up, he said to me, "I've done a lot of bad things in my life, really bad things. I ruined my son's life and he's in jail, and the people I've hurt the most have been the kindest to me." My heart went out to him and I held his hands in mine as I prayed for God to give him peace. He cried.

I spoke to the other nurses about his despair and one said to me, "Don't you know who your patient is? He's the grand Dragon of the Ku Klux Klan!" I was stunned! That sweet man, those blue eyes. He was going to be tried for his past crimes. Still, my heart went out to him, for I sensed his deep remorse, and I passed no judgment on him. I thought no judgment or punishment was worse than the sentence he had placed upon himself. It seems my kindness to him must have been ripping away at his heart. I did not mention the KKK to him and continued to comfort and care for him as before. His anguish was obvious to anyone who took the time to see, and I could not help but feel empathy for him. I was better able to understand Matthew 5:44: *"But I say unto you, love your enemies, bless them that curse you, do good to them that hate you, and pray for them which despitefully use you and persecute you..."* (KJV). It was freeing to me to feel genuine love and compassion for this man who once hated me, sight unseen, but who could not now love himself.

Racial prejudice was present when Jesus walked this earth. In one of his devotionals, Oswald Chambers mentions the animosity and "racial prejudice" of the Samaritans toward Jesus, a Jew. Yet the Lord had one of his best-known conversations with a Samaritan woman he met at Jacob's well. He taught his disciples to do good to those who hate you. That was an easy command to obey when I first looked into eyes the color blue of a pristine sea.

Consider the Lilies

LAURA BRADFORD

"If that is how God clothes the grass of the field, which is here today, and tomorrow is thrown into the fire, how much more will he clothe you, O you of little faith!"

Luke 12:27-28, NIV

As another parched summer day came to an end, I went outside to give my gardens an extra drink of water.

Normally, I'd enjoy those few moments of lingering in the twilight, but worries about money were weighing me down. I'd just finished reviewing the financial status of my widowed mother-in-law's accounts and my own. With Mom in an expensive Alzheimer's facility, it appeared she'd outlive her money. Since I'm a widow too, I wondered if I'd suffer the same fate. How could I make my money last? Should I quit giving to charity? Quit using the air conditioner? Quit watering the yard?

I knew I couldn't let my gardens die.

In the fading sunset, the colors of my flowers took on a surreal glow. Trees whispered a lullaby, while the cooling breeze embraced me in a gentle caress. How could I let all this wither and die? The very thought broke my heart.

This was my sanctuary—a place to meet with the Lord in the cool of the evening—a place to escape a crazed, self-adoring world, and imagine Eden. Everything here bore the Lord's signature. To quote Paul from Romans 1:20, *"God's invisible qualities"* (NIV) were displayed in the vast array of colors, in the bountiful crops, even in the crescent moon smiling down at me. Faint chirpings of sleepy birds seemed to confirm, "All is well. God is here." But worries kept me from receiving comfort from their evensong.

Dragging my garden hose to a flowerbed, I swept water over the mass of color. As leaves and petals danced under the droplets, I noticed a few tall leaves parting to reveal a stranger in my garden—a new flower.

"What are you doing here?" I asked, dropping the hose to have a better look.

I stared in disbelief as a pink calla lily swayed gracefully on her stalk, like a royal matron, surrounded by her entourage of petunias.

But I hadn't planted a lily there! To me, lilies were a waste of money, blooming only briefly before they shrivel and die. But, there she stood, a tall lady wrapped in a delicate pink cape.

As I gazed in awe, Jesus' own words came to me. *"Consider how the lilies grow. They do not labor or spin. Yet I tell you, not even Solomon in all his splendor was dressed like one of these. If that is how God clothes the grass of the field, which is here today, and tomorrow is thrown into the fire, how much more will he clothe you, O you of little faith!"* (Luke 12:27-28, NIV).

Joy replaced worry as the truth of those verses soaked into my soul. The miracle lily's silent message convicted me of trusting dollars rather than trusting God! How foolish to doubt the One who'd taken care of me since childhood! He'd always been there, through illnesses, losses, and lean times. He wasn't about to abandon me now.

Tears poured down my face … inching around a smile of relief. Without my asking, without my believing, God had sent a messenger of peace, a sign of his power! If he was capable of planting this lily to bloom exactly when I needed it, wasn't he also capable of meeting every need, at any time, in any form?

A week passed since I had found the lily. She's still standing tall, waving on the breezes. Evidently, she was determined to show off her beauty until I fully understood the Lord's promise, *"… I am with you always, to the very end of the age"* (Matthew 28:20, NIV).

This Race Is Not Just for The Runners

MULENGA MUNDENDE

"...And let us run with endurance the race God has set before us. We do this by keeping our eyes on Jesus, the champion who initiates and perfects our faith."

Hebrews 12:1-2a, NLT

I look forward to spring with great anticipation. Spring brings the beauty of budding trees, sweet-smelling flowers, warm sunshine, and scents of freshly mowed grass. Spring ushers in the time to train outdoors for competitive running races. I have run several half-marathons and 5Ks. I run these races with all my strength, not expecting to win any, but to improve on my previous time, enjoy myself, and cross the finish line.

I developed iliotibial band syndrome on both knees when I was training for my second half marathon. I became the poster child for what not to do when training because I did everything wrong. I increased my mileage too fast, did not wear proper shoes, did not rest adequately between runs, stretch properly, or listen to my body. When I ran or walked, I felt excruciating pain that felt as if my knees were being stabbed by a hot, sharp knife. I had never experienced anything like that before. I was forced to halt training two weeks prior to the race.

It was a dark, rainy day when the race started. I was feeling pretty well until the middle of the first mile, when the pain returned, not as excruciating as before, but agonizing enough to slow me down tremendously. The pain removed the fun from the race and shattered my goal of beating my previous time. All I wanted to do then was cross the finish line.

I was challenged mentally and physically. When the pain got worse, I threw myself a pity party. The rain and pain frustrated me. I was not excited about the people who were passing me and running with ease. Wasn't it just easier to stop and call a cab? Then it hit me. Focusing on my pain was not helping matters. I decided to recite one of my favorite Bible verses: *"I can do all things through Christ, who gives me strength"* (Philippians 4:13, NLT).

As I repeatedly said this verse, something miraculous happened. God gave me strength and opened my heart and eyes. I saw people of different shapes, physical conditions, and nationalities; all running at different levels. Some speed walked, leisurely walked, jogged, or sprinted. I remembered the lyrics from Cindy Morgan's song "Take My Life": "This race is not just for the runners, some of us walk while others barely crawl," and found them to be appropriate, meaningful, and applicable at that moment.

I looked on the sidelines and saw friends, family members, and volunteers who had woken up early to cheer us on and provide physical nourishment. Looking around, I saw, as if for the first time, my earthly father who had been running beside me the whole race, cheering me on.

I have often reflected on that experience. I learned that we are in a spiritual race, running at different levels of our spirituality, building relationships with our heavenly Father, while seeking and doing his will as the Holy Spirit convicts us. When life throws different challenges at us, we need to cling to God's mighty arms. Surrounded by other men and women, we will do well if we shift the focus from us to them, being their cheerleaders, offering our time, providing an encouraging word, or meeting their physical needs. Most importantly, we should focus our attention on our Savior and Lord. We will do well to remember that our Heavenly Father is with us every step of the way, encouraging, supporting, and carrying us when we cannot go any farther. As the champion of champions, he initiates and perfects our faith. He will see us through to the finish line. If he cannot remove the challenge, he will provide the strength to overcome it.

"Therefore, since we are surrounded by such a huge crowd of witnesses to the life of faith, let us strip off every weight that slows us down, especially the sin that so easily trips us up. And let us run with endurance the race God has set before us. We do this by keeping our eyes on Jesus, the champion who initiates and perfects our faith" (Hebrews 12:1-2a, NLT).

Seven Years of Bad...
Seven Years of Plenty

CYNTHIA MERCER

"Delight thyself also in the Lord: and he shall give thee the desires of thine heart."

Psalm 37:4, KJV

My morning began like most other days, except this particular day I longed for some answers from God and had decided the night before I would spend the day fasting and praying as I waited on what God wanted to reveal to me. So as I made my way up to the operating room I asked God to put someone in my path that day I could show his love to as well.

That early October morning, it was obvious that my first patient was extremely nervous about her scheduled operation. She had a very familiar face and she seemed to recognize me as well. As we began to visit, we realized that we did know each other from a home school coalition group I had attended earlier in the year. She was very relieved that I was going to be her nurse and she began to cry and express to me her concerns about the surgery she was about to have. I had just asked her if I could pray for her, when a friend of hers approached the bedside and my patient began to cry even more intensely as she expressed her sadness that her husband wasn't a believer. I sensed she was very hurt, since her tears went beyond the fact that she was having surgery that day.

I asked if I could pray for her, and as I prayed it was obvious that she was very burdened down that day. As I said, "Amen," her tears seemed to fade away and she thanked me for the kind words and the prayer.

Immediately following our prayer, the Holy Spirit prompted me to share with her my story about my husband's conversion experience seven years earlier. I explained that when I had married him, I was sure I had found the man of my dreams … only to discover a few months later that he was an alcoholic, and addicted to pornography, cocaine, and crystal meth as well. I was extremely distraught and confused. I had two choices, one being to leave and file for a divorce; the other being to stay and pray and watch God perform a miracle! One morning in my quiet time, the Holy Spirit impressed me that if I were to leave, I would miss out on the testimony that God wanted to give me. So, I chose to stay and let God have his way with me.

I began to fast and pray for my husband. It wasn't an overnight process and there were many tears and sleepless nights as I agonized in prayer for him. I encouraged her to not give up on praying for her husband. It dawned on me at about the moment I began to pray for her that it had been fourteen years since my husband and I had married and that although the first seven years were extremely difficult times, the last seven years had been incredible! I rejoiced as I shared with her how God had answered my prayers. My husband not only became a believer; he became a pastor!

The concern and tears left her face and were replaced with a smile instead. I wheeled her cart into the operating room with a bit of a smile on my face and heart as well. I was thankful for the divine appointment that God had given me that day for a prayer and words of encouragement to a troubled precious soul.

Waiting for Morning

ALICIA BRUXVOORT

"For his anger lasts only a moment, but his favor lasts a lifetime; weeping may remain for a night, but rejoicing comes in the morning."

Psalm 30:5, NIV

I hear the pitter-patter of his sleepy feet before his voice wakes me. I don't need to look at the clock on my bedside table. I know it reads 3 AM. This is his waking time. His squinty eyes and slurred speech confirm that he's not rested, but according to the odd rhythm of my three-year-old son's sleep pattern, daylight should have already arrived.

He tugs at my arm, and asks, "Is it morning yet?"

"No buddy," I whisper, trying not to wake his exhausted daddy beside me. "It's still dark outside."

A shrill moan slips from his lips. "When will morning come?" "When the darkness disappears," I remind him.

Reluctantly, I roll from bed and grab his slender hand. Like every other night, we walk across the hallway to the room where his big brother sleeps. I nudge my littlest boy into the bottom bunk, pull his special blanket to his chin, and kiss him goodnight again.

"Stay by me and pray for me," he pleads. I glance at my cozy bed across the hall.

"Please, Mommy, just *one* minute." I crawl carefully beside him and place my hands on his head of tousled hair. I breathe in deeply his sleepy smell and remind myself that this child won't be little forever.

"Dear Lord," I murmur so as not to wake my firstborn snoring above us. "Wrap your mighty arms around Joshua. Keep him safe. Command your angels to stand guard over this boy, your treasure..." I speak softly the Scripture that comes to mind. I rub his warm bony back. I listen to the steady pulse of his breathing. I try not to think about my own cramped legs wedged into the crack between his bed and the wall. I whisper assurance that morning will, indeed, arrive. And I empathize with his impatience. No matter how old we grow, it is difficult to wait in darkness.

I've asked my heavenly Father countless times when morning would come. As I've hovered crib-side and listened for the belabored breathing of my struggling newborn; as I've battled mammoth discouragement and wondered if God even cares; as I've listened to the anxious voice on the phone, "your sister's in the hospital again." Such moments are the nighttimes of the soul. Darkness makes dawn seem so far away.

In her book, *Calm My Anxious Heart,* Linda Dillow reminds us that *"faith is walking in the dark with God, holding his hand."* Savor her insightful commentary on a familiar Bible story. *"In the book of Exodus, we find the children of Israel camped by the edge of the Red Sea. It was night, pitch black except for the pillar of fire God had placed between his people and the Egyptians. Can you imagine their fear? "Hidden in the text is the tiny phrase, 'All that night the LORD drove the sea back'* (Exodus 14:21, NIV).... *Because it was night, they couldn't see what the 'wind of God' was accomplishing on their behalf.... [But in the morning] they walked on dry ground to freedom."* [1]

When we find ourselves in the nighttime of life, we are wise to remember that God is working even when we can't see. Just as he intervened "all that night," for his chosen people while they clung to one another in fear, he is faithfully at work in our darkness, too.

My small son's sluggish snores eventually bring my prayers to a close. Silently, I slip my hands out from under his sleeping head and return to the comforts of my own bed. The sky is still black, but the frogs and the crickets sing a rowdy song of hope beyond my window.

They know morning is on its way. Or perhaps they are watching the Creator of the stars work wonders in the darkness.

As for me, I'll have to wait for morning.

1 Linda Dillow. *Calm My Anxious Heart: A Woman's Guide to Finding Contentment* (Colorado Springs, NavPress, 2007), 151.

Pushing Through Life

STEPHANIE LIND

"…do not be anxious about anything, but in everything by prayer and supplication with thanksgiving let your requests be made known to God. And the peace of God, which surpasses all understanding, will guard your hearts and your minds in Christ Jesus."

Philippians 4:6-7, ESV

Some days it feels like all I do is push…

Push the snooze button (okay, twice). Push my way through morning traffic. Push to get more things done in a day. Even push the limits on the minimum amount of sleep time!

Why so much pushing? Society seems to have the view that more is better… so we push.

One morning as I pushed open an office door, a friend walking through must have seen the stressed look on my face and simply said: "PUSH… Pray Until Something Happens." She just mentioned it casually as the door had PUSH written on the handlebar, but her simple acronym really got me thinking. How often do I push through life, trying to direct my own path and getting frustrated in the process? In reality, I should PUSH as soon as my alarm goes off. I should PUSH for peace during my morning commute. I should PUSH all throughout my day.

I work in a hospital. In this setting, there can be a lot of physical pushing–pushing patients in wheelchairs, pushing lifesaving medicine through a patient's IV, pushing our keyboards while typing up the next great business proposal. And just think of all those women in labor and delivery; there is a lot of pushing in that unit! Each of these pushing opportunities around us can provide a silent reminder to pray. Pray until something happens.

Is there more pushing than peace of mind in your life? Perhaps you find yourself pushing day-to-day more than you might wish? You may feel pressured by trying to manage a tight family budget, or balancing the demands of being a loving wife, mother, cook, pet supervisor, house cleaner, charitable volunteer, calendar manager, cheerleader-in-chief, chauffeur, and organizer of multiple activities, from Christmas parties to birthday parties, and everything in between. As a result, at the end of many days, there seems to be not enough time or energy for yourself, your spouse, or your relationship with the Lord.

One of my favorite Scripture passages says, *"Are you tired? Worn out? Burned out on religion? Come* to me. Get away with me and you'll recover your life. I'll show you how to take a real rest. Walk with me and work with me—watch how I do it. Learn the unforced rhythms of grace. I won't lay anything heavy or ill-fitting on you. Keep company with me and you'll learn to live freely and lightly"* (Matthew 11:28-30, MSG).

"*Learn the unforced rhythms of grace.*" Unforced. My life is part of God's plan, which is therefore a recipient of unforced, pure grace. If it had a label it would read, "No pushing necessary!" I don't have to try to force things to happen, because he is in charge.

Can you feel the hug from God around you? If God is by my side each step of the way, he will show me how to live "freely and lightly." The burden of having to manage it all is gone. I can "cease striving" and stop pushing and just rest in knowing that he is God. I wonder what would happen if every time we pushed, we PUSHED as well?

The Master Gardener

DIANE THURBER

"But I trust in you Lord; I say, You are my God."

Psalm 31:14, NIV

This spring my gracious neighbors invited me to share garden space with them. I was excited, because gardening in their 10-foot-high fenced-in space promised protection from most critters for my tender plants and developing produce. It also offered four-foot raised beds for gardening ease with timers for automatic watering morning and afternoon, screens to keep the menacing birds away, and a greenhouse with regulated temperature, automatic watering, and classical music to help my plants thrive.

When the *Farmer's Almanac* said it was optimal time to plant, I drove to the amazing, award-winning Tagawa Gardens where master gardeners and gardener-wannabes like me come from near and far to explore 160,000 square feet of heirloom seeds, organic fertilizers that promise to double plant size or yield, and unusual species of vegetables and culinary herbs. In fact, this spring they offered sixteen varieties of garlic!

Soon my shopping cart was loaded with more than I came for–tender plants, seeds, insect spray, string and trellises. I left Tagawa Gardens with increased confidence after coaching and encouragement from their well-educated gardening team.

After allowing sufficient time for my delicate plants to adjust from the shaded, protective indoor nursery to their new outdoor environment with piercing sunrays and brisk winds, I lovingly deposited my treasures in the rich garden soil.

I've gardened before, but this year my garden was the most effortless creation I've ever tended. In years past, I toiled over hardened dirt mixed with clay that sprouted weeds of countless varieties to prepare a place to deposit my investment, and each time hoped for a surplus yield. I was often disappointed. But not this year. With optimum soil, well water without chemical additives that soaked the roots, and natural fertilizer from the neighbor's horse stable, I realized I actually did very little to produce the bountiful harvest that included sweet corn, broccoli, lettuce, eggplant, basil, succulent cantaloupe, juicy watermelon, tomatoes, okra, tender peas, and peppers.

As I tended my little garden space, I had time to reflect about my Master gardener who guards and guides the less-than-suitable soil of my heart. I thought about how he longs to nourish me so I'll lovingly turn to the Son and flourish like my vegetables; but sometimes, I stubbornly cling to selfish ambition like my sugar peas that reach out for nearby veggies instead of the trellis I carefully placed near them for support. The pea plants wrap themselves around the shorter vegetables nearby, and their growth is stunted. I do that sometimes, too, thinking I know a better plan than my Master gardener. And my growth is stunted. And then I can feel my Master gardener gently pruning and redirecting my life when I ask him to.

Like the fertilizer I blended with the rich soil to strengthen my little plants, my Master Gardener longs to enrich me with the nutrients he deposits in his manual for my happiness, the Bible. As I read, I find this book has so many lessons designed to help me grow to my fullest potential as he designed.

And then there's the insect spray. There were so many varieties of bugs and worms just waiting to dine on my endless buffet, and they threatened to reduce the plants to mere stubs. As I did my best to ward off these menacing species, it was sometimes a losing battle. I am thankful for my Master gardener who never sleeps nor slumbers, who sends his angels to camp round about me to keep me in all my ways. What peace this brings me!

I've learned it's all about trust. My Master gardener wants me to submit to him, so he can lovingly lead and guide me to be all he dreams for me to be. It's a partnership. He doesn't force me, but when I stray he patiently waits for me to let him be the Master gardener again. When I encounter unanticipated dangers, he's there to protect. My job is to trust. Simply trust.

The View from 26 Weeks

JAMIE SANTA CRUZ

> *"… as a bridegroom rejoices over his bride,
> so will your God rejoice over you."*
>
> **Isaiah 62:5b, NIV**

We are newlyweds, my husband and I, young at love and head over heels for each other. So much so, in fact, that the whiteboard on our refrigerator is still updated each Friday with a fresh count of the number of weeks we've been married. "25" it reads now, but tomorrow, Daniel will rub out that number and replace it with a "26" in fresh black script.

Six months? Has the time really flown so quickly?

We didn't get here easily. In fact, the first time we met, through an introduction by mutual friends three years ago, Daniel was cold to romance. Women were best avoided at all costs, or so his thinking went. We did not keep in touch.

But a year later, when by happenstance we met for the second time, he felt differently. Perhaps it was something about the Christmastime air, but for whatever magical reason, he was interested. This time, phone calls followed. I was intrigued, though unfortunately by then I was just beginning a new relationship with someone else. Again Daniel and I parted ways, but he told me to call if things didn't work out.

Spring came and went, and by June it was clear that indeed, things were not going to work out. I was alone again. Daniel, too, was still alone. Was he still interested? I didn't know, but my tentative phone call yielded a positive response: Yes, he was interested.

Third time's a charm, they say. Somewhere between Christmas and New Year's, on a crisp, star-studded evening, he told me that he was going to marry me someday. I giggled. By then, I knew that when he asked, I would say yes.

Our wedding was in May five months later—a simple affair in a beautiful Civil War-era painted white church, at sundown on a Friday evening and with lanterns in the windows. Despite the trials and obstacles that remain constant in life, every day since then has been sweeter than those that came before.

Today, half a year removed from our exchange of vows, I am stirring bean soup at the stove and trying to remember how much chili powder goes into the recipe, when I am jolted from my concentration as Daniel pokes his head into the kitchen.

"Mi amor!" he calls to me, a boyish grin lighting his face. He sweeps into the kitchen, and I can't help laughing as he whisks me off my feet and twirls me around the room. When he sets me back on the floor, he takes my hand and leads me in an impromptu dance, for which neither of us knows the steps. Soon we are tripping over each other's feet and collapsing, laughing and out of breath, into each other's arms.

"Tesoro de mi corazón," he whispers into my ear, drawing my head to his chest. He is teaching me Spanish, his native language, but we joke that his approach is a little impractical for the real world, as my schooling in the romantic vocabulary of the language is far outpacing more usable vocabulary. But never mind that. I know I am loved, and I wouldn't trade that for perfect Spanish fluency.

Entering into this new stage of life with my husband has brought a fresh understanding of what the love of God must be like. After all, in the Bible, it is God who is presented as a bridegroom and we, his people, are the object of his desire, whom he pursues with ardor and tender concern. The authors of both the Old and New Testaments draw on the imagery of the love of a man for a woman as one of the best earthly insights into the intensity of God's passion for his people (e.g., Hosea 1-3; 2 Corinthians 11:2; Revelation 21:2).

Now that I have been a bride, I comprehend this divine love a little better. Every time I fall into my husband's embrace or shiver under the tender touch of his fingers, I sense more clearly the love God feels for me.

And all I can say is this: if the love I share with Daniel is at all comparable to the love God has for us, how sweet must be God's love.

A Worthy Resolution

HELEN HEAVIRLAND

"Be still and know that I am God…"
Psalm 46:10, KJV

Ding-dong.

Tense and tired of interruptions, I trudged toward the door. Treasured out-of-state friends greeted me. My husband heard and hurried from a back room.

The hellos and what's-happenings buzzed back and forth while we and our nature-loving friends drank in the view from our hilltop home. In the few minutes we visited, thirty delicately designed California quail, topknots bouncing, scratched and pecked at our porch-side bird restaurant. A sparrow hawk surveyed the lower pasture from a fence post. Two bronze-breasted, ring-necked pheasant roosters strutted across the snow. Mallards swam in the stream below. Oregon juncos arrived and flitted and feasted among the quail.

I hadn't seen that many birds in weeks. I started to say so when a hawk soared by just *below* us. We "oohed" and "aahed"—what a treat to look down on the miracle of flight, to see pinions flutter in the updraft, to watch the hawk's head turn from side to side as he sought supper.

One of those "aha" moments burst upon me. *You haven't seen many birds lately because you've not sat still and looked.*

Our friends soon continued their journey. My husband went to work. Lost in thought, I laundered and cleaned.

Lately, employment and errands, cooking and cleaning, church-going and bill-paying, family, friends, and crises had demanded my attention. Weeks had appeared and whooshed away at a dizzying pace.

A poster I'd seen popped into mind. Piles of paperwork covered a desktop and overflowed onto the floor. Nearly hidden behind the clutter, a frazzle-haired, bleary-eyed woman stared at the chaos. I could almost hear her drone the caption, "The hurrier I go, the behinder I get."

My own life seemed to overflow the bounds of twenty-four-hour days. Last week had cast its leftovers into yesterday. Yesterday had heaved its unfinished tasks helter-skelter into today.

I thought back to a previous home. Life had pressured and prodded me then as much as now.

Perhaps more. But there I'd learned that otters don't schedule appointments to frolic in the river. That rainbows disappear. That gorgeous wood ducks don't ring the doorbell and ask if you want to see them. I'd learned to take minute vacations—to stop and look at a cloud formation, to listen to rain patter or pound the roof, to be cheered by a chickadee at the bird feeder.

I had learned that these pauses to appreciate the common or the spectacular did not decrease my productivity. Instead, minute vacations with the created and the Creator relaxed and energized me. They empowered me to accomplish more. They helped me maintain a peace that improved the quality of life for me . . . and those nearby.

Pressure to do more and be more had crowded out my minute vacations. I didn't know just when I'd allowed it. But I was tired. I dared not wait for rest till some far-off holiday. As I passed an east window, movement in the snow-covered field caught my attention. *What's that?* I wondered.

My momentum moved me on. Then . . . I consciously chose to lay down my armload of clean clothes and get started on a worthy resolution. I fetched binoculars. In the year we'd lived here, we'd observed hundreds of geese fly over but we'd not seen any settle where we could observe them. Now a dozen Canada geese gabbled and fed just a hundred yards from our window.

After just moments of watching nature, I felt refreshed, because I had been reminded to: *"Be still and know that I am God..."* (Psalm 46:10, KJV).

The Gift of Choice

DELORES FRANCOIS

> "What man is he that feareth the Lord? him shall he teach in the way that he shall choose. His soul shall dwell at ease; and his seed shall inherit the earth."
>
> **Psalm 25:12-13, KJV**

It was on a Friday evening in October 1992, when I received the call from my sister, Beverly, that our father had passed way. She wanted to know my plans for the funeral. I told her that I would not be attending. Why in the world would I want to go to the funeral of a stranger? He had abandoned us when we were children and I still remembered the day he left. He had told Beverly and I that he was going away to get a job in another town and that he would return and get us. He never returned.

Beverly always loved our father and I believe she always saw him for who he could have been. I have always liked that about her. Even though he had abandoned us, she chose to love him as if he was always there being the best father there was. Later in life, she would always encourage me to call and say hello to him and let him know what was going on in my life. Sometimes I would. Most times I would not.

My father was an alcoholic. As a child, I remember his friends bringing him home so drunk he literally passed out on the floor. My mother was so frustrated that she kept hitting him with a big wooden stick trying to wake him up. He would not move. I remember thinking that he was dead. How scary of a memory is that for a child! But not all my memories of my father were scary. I can remember running down the street with Beverly to greet him upon his return from work each evening. He would pick the both of us up at the same time and hug us!

My father's absence affected our family deeply. He had left us so vulnerable. There were so many things that happened in my life that I attribute to him not being there. The one thing that stands out most in my mind was the strangers who came in and out of our lives, taking advantage of my mom and silently hurting her children, especially her daughters. We were changed undeniably forever because of it. We bear the deep scars, some hidden and some not so hidden.

God in his divine wisdom gave each of us the power of choice. My father and our family suffered the consequences of his choices. I certainly have made choices in my life that I am not proud of. They have affected me and others. Most importantly, I realize that my choices have eternal consequences. I am so happy that God forgives us when we make bad decisions. It is my earnest prayer that God will direct me as I strive to do better with the choices I make each day.

Two days after Beverly's call, I changed my mind and made the choice to attend my father's funeral. I am so happy I did! After all, he was my father and the only one I had in this world. Beverly and I were the only two out of our six siblings who attended. We learned from relatives who cared for him during his illness that in his heart he had never abandoned us. He spoke of us often and shared his memories of us over and over again. It meant so much to us to know that!

It has been eighteen years since my father's death. When I speak of him, even today, it brings tears to my eyes and I feel like a little girl again wanting my father to sweep me up in his arms again! Today, I choose to remember how much my father loved me. I choose to forgive and not to live with bitterness.

Choice is a power and a privilege our heavenly Father has given all of us. What will you do with yours?

"All the paths of the Lord are mercy and truth unto such as keep his covenant and his testimonies. For thy name's sake, O Lord, pardon mine iniquity; for it is great. What man is he that feareth the Lord? him shall he teach in the way that he shall choose. His soul shall dwell at ease; and his seed shall inherit the earth" (Psalm 25:10-13, KJV).

Somersaults in the Sky

TERRI CRUZE

"...I have come that they may have life, and have it to the full."
John 10:10, NIV

I love to go hiking! At the mere mention of the word, I almost begin to drool as I run for my shoes: "A hike? When? Where? What are we waiting for? Let's go!" I feel so close to God, so connected to life, when I am hiking. It isn't that I think God is any closer to me on a hike; it's more like I'm less distracted and more tuned-in to his presence, and my heart is more available to his touch.

When I am at home or at work, I tend to focus on the minute details of the tasks before me. A thousand things run through my head all at the same time, like a whirlwind: *What did I leave unfinished yesterday? What am I going to make for dinner? Don't forget to stop at the store and pick up some bread and milk. Did I tell my family that I love them before I left this morning?*

When I am out in the woods or up on a mountain, however, I leave the distractions behind. I am there, alone with God, with the evidence of his love, his beauty, and his creativity all around me. I can't get enough of it! I guess I am a hike-aholic—but it works for me.

One particular afternoon hike stands out in my mind: I was out with my kids and a few friends on one of the mountains near my home in the Pacific Northwest. It was a bit windy that day, but the sun was out, and the sky was clear. The views from the ridge we were following were breathtaking! I was just imagining what we would be able to see when we got to the top—probably twenty miles in any direction from that lofty vantage point—when suddenly, something to our left grabbed my attention. What caught my eye was a group of about eight or ten large, black birds, vultures I thought, several hundred feet above a cliff. I was intrigued by what they were doing.

They were lined up in a row at the top of the cliff, and, one at a time, they were falling forward into the wind and performing all kinds of aerobatic flips and dives and somersaults in the air. Of course, it is not unusual for birds to dive and circle around in the sky, but these birds just seemed to be having so much fun doing it! They weren't searching for food or following a migration path. They weren't working at all, as far as I could tell. They were just taking time off and enjoying themselves.

I must admit, for a moment I was a bit envious. But as I stood watching them tumble and soar, I couldn't help feeling a little more lighthearted myself. I felt joy growing inside me as I watched them and imagined myself joining them. How exhilarating the wind must feel rushing by as they dove over the edge, their wings catching the air just right and sending them flying back up, high above the cliff. How free they must feel! As I left them and continued with my own journey, I began to walk with a little more spring in my step and inhaled a little deeper.

The Spirit moved me to wonder: *Is this how my heavenly Father feels when he sees me fully experiencing life? Does he put his arm around my shoulder and say, "Yes! That's it! Go ahead, have fun. Take it all in! I made this for you; do you like it?"*

Then it hit me! This is what Jesus must have meant when he said, *"...I have come that they may have life, and have it to the full"* (John 10:10, NIV). He did not tell us that if we are good enough, or if we somehow qualified, he would send a select few of us a special blessing of joy. No, he was very clear that he came to give each of us an abundant, joyful life. We can have it, right here and right now. No strings attached, if we simply accept it. What an awesome gift!

Never More Than You Can Handle

SHARON JALLAD

"The temptations in your life are no different from what others experience. And God is faithful. He will not allow the temptation to be more than you can stand. When you are tempted, he will show you a way out so that you can endure."

1 Corinthians 10:13, NLT

When the phone rang late one evening in 2007 and my father's home number flashed on the caller ID, my immediate response was a mix of anxiety and dread. A phone call from his night nurse usually meant that something was wrong. My experience after six years of being my father's legal guardian told me it could be a number of urgent things—either Dad had fallen again, his blood pressure was too high, or he was out of diapers. While I knew that I could not and would not ignore the ringing plea for assistance, there were times when the phone rang that I wished to escape. Like many women, I found myself stretched between being a wife, a mother of two children, a full-time insurance executive, and caring for my infirm father.

As I feared, the dreaded phone call that night turned out to be more serious than a request for adult diapers. Dad was prone to falling. He had suffered a debilitating stroke in 2003 which left him paralyzed on his right side and aphasic. His limited mobility was shaky at best even when supported by the arms of caregivers and a sturdy cane. Always determined, however, to flex some independence, on that night, Dad had attempted to walk without assistance to the bathroom and had fallen backward, splitting his head open on the sharp corner of a bookcase.

Thank God for 911 and first responders!

After reciting from memory a list of current medications and my father's medical history over the phone to the paramedics, I nervously agreed to meet the ambulance at the hospital's emergency room. Visits to the hospital had become as routine as getting the kids off to school—grab a sweater, a book, a snack, and my cell phone. I knew the drill well and prepared for the long hours ahead.

After a marathon night of medical forms, tests, and uncertainty, the doctors admitted my father for further treatment. The sun was coming up and the night shift headed off-duty, when I finally wandered sleepily to the parking lot. In the quiet of my car, overcome by fatigue and worry, I began to cry. *How could I continue to care for my father and juggle the rest of my life?* I wondered. I was not sure I had the strength or the courage. Then, as I was driving home, a strange sense of release came over me and I realized that I was exactly where I was supposed to be in my life, that God had put me in that place so that I could give my father the care that he needed.

I had a loving husband who gave me support.
I had a job that allowed me flexible time-off.
I was blessed with good health to sustain me.

My father passed away in December 2007. The responsibility of caring for him, while never easy, opened my heart and blessed my life in so many unexpected ways. I cherish the time I spent with him and the love that bound us especially during the most difficult moments of his declining health. The journey was emotionally and physically exhausting, but along the way I continued to be comforted in knowing that God knew in advance what would be required of me and how much I could handle.

Perfectly Planned

LIZBETH FERNANDEZ

"You made all the delicate, inner parts of my body and knit me together in my mother's womb. Thank you for making me so wonderfully complex!"

Psalm 139:13-14, NLT

All little girls dream of the day when they will get married and have a child of their own. We play dress up with our mother's clothes and have pretend weddings where Daddy is the groom. Our mothers buy us baby dolls with all of the cute, matching accessories to help us care for our new child. Everything is planned and everything is Perfect.

As an adult, my dreams were the same. I wanted to get married and start a family, have a child of my own. Finally my day came and it was time for me to get married. Everything was planned and everything was Perfect. It wasn't long before I wanted to achieve my next dream of having a child. I was excited and nervous all at the same time when I found out I had conceived. This was Perfect...until something went wrong and I learned that I had miscarried. The pain of losing what I wanted so badly seemed unbearable. Everyone said that there was a reason and that I could try again, but all I could think of was, *But I wanted THIS baby.*

My desire to have a child intensified. Two more times I conceived and two more times I experienced the loss. Why was this happening to me? What did I do so wrong that God gave me life and yet it was taken from me? Why didn't I deserve to have the one thing I so desperately wanted?

Years passed and my dream and desire to have a baby resurfaced. This time, my husband and I planned it … Perfectly.

One beautiful spring day in March, I learned that I was pregnant. I was adamant on doing everything right to ensure that nothing went wrong and I'd hold my baby in my arms nine months later. Thirteen weeks later something bad happened and I thought I was losing my baby. *Dear God, no not again,* is all I could think of. *Please don't do this to me again,* I pleaded.

My body began to take on a new shape and my belly began to grow. I began feeling something that felt like butterfly wings tickling my belly from the inside and I soon learned that those flutters were my baby moving inside of me. I later learned that I was having a girl. I was so excited that I couldn't wait to design her nursery in beautiful shades of lavender and pink, butterflies stenciled on the walls, stuffed animals delicately placed all around, everything so Perfect.

Weeks later I learned that something was wrong with the baby. "There's a fifty percent chance that she has Down Syndrome," they said. "We can do a test to be sure, but we must do it quickly so that you have time to terminate." It was one blow right after the other. I didn't plan this. There goes my Perfect dream, my Perfect baby.

I finally gave birth to my little girl and when I first laid eyes on her beautiful face and looked into her eyes, my outlook changed. This was My baby, the baby that I longed for, the baby that fought to be here, the baby that God wanted me to have. God did not punish me. I had not done anything wrong. He needed someone to unconditionally love and care for his angel and he thought so highly of Me that he chose Me to be her mother. I had to lose what I wanted most, to see and feel so blessed with the gift I had been given.

"You made all the delicate, inner parts of my body and knit me together in my mother's womb. Thank you for making me so wonderfully complex!" (Psalm 139:13-14, NLT).

We are all made in God's image.

Adam is missing a rib so that a masterpiece known as a woman could be created. My daughter is God's masterpiece and his most precious gift to me. She is wonderfully made. She was his plan and she is Perfect! And so are you!

Forgiving Daddy, Healing Me

BETTY KOSSICK

"…bearing with one another, and forgiving one another… even as Christ forgave you, so you must also do."

Colossians 3:13, NKJV

As a child, a hard-scrabble existence dogged my steps. My divorced mom struggled at menial jobs to keep us housed and fed. That scenario started for me at age ten. Previously, I had lived for five years in a children's care home. The five years before that, after my babyhood, I often hid in a built-in bookcase to escape my parent's arguments. I stopped my ears, trying not to hear mom's screams, both at him for his drunkenness or because of him battering her.

Hugging my cat proved comforting to me. I told him about the ugliness. I did not have a grandparent or anyone to hold me and say, "I'm sorry" or "I love you." I hated it all. When I saw other girls skipping down the street, holding their daddy's hand, I yearned to be one of them. I did not bellyache to my school chums about my lot. Nor did I reveal the home sadness to my teachers. In those days, family secrets stayed in the closet.

Like many others during the Great American Depression we possessed little, and when daddy guzzled from the bottle, we had less. His drinking cronies gave him a sense of camaraderie. Life proved difficult. However, I was not a crybaby about it all. I tried, in my youthful way, to overcome the ugliness surrounding me, in fact, to the point of pretense.

After a severe beating, Mom finally said, "enough" to the miserable life that living with an alcoholic brings and we walked away. Life did not turn into a fairyland existence. In fact, hardship persisted, but the abuse that comes with "life in a bottle" ceased.

Even though I tried to hide it all, I think some of my teachers knew. I still have my second-grade report card on which my teacher wrote, "One of the nicest little girls in the school." Those few words helped me feel special.

At age twelve, I started on my journey with God–hunting for him! Little did I realize that he was the heart-hunter. Six years of searching brought me into a personal knowledge of Jesus as my Lord and Savior, at age eighteen. I discovered that I was created in God's image and he was my Father. I cannot tell you the day or the hour, but along the way, I forgave my earthly father for depriving me of his love, a happy childhood, and my basic needs. If Jesus could forgive those who crucified him, I certainly *must* forgive my dad. I threw away all the passionate feelings of despair that had accumulated in me as a child because of his behavior.

Over the years, I saw him—even visited him in jail—but the encounters were usually stifled, mostly because he reeked of liquor. Because of these awkward meetings (some were downright fall-over-drunk times with him and his new wife, another alcoholic), I never told him that I forgave him—that is until my mother died.

The telephone rang across the two-hundred miles that separated us that December afternoon. When I answered it, I heard my father's voice, "Betty Ann, I'm sorry about your mom." He asked a few questions, and I answered. Then he astounded me saying, "I'm sorry that I wasn't the father I should have been."

He had mellowed in his old age and if he smelled of the bottle, I was not exposed to the reek of it—but hearing the words finalized the forgiveness I felt toward him. I told him, "It is okay now, Dad. Mom and I had a tough life. There were times when we did not have anything except canned green beans and black coffee for a meal. We could not buy coal for the furnace. Life hurt. Yet when I accepted Jesus Christ as Lord of my life, I asked Jesus to forgive me of my sins and along the way, I also forgave you."

He thanked me. Four months later he, too, died.

Domestic abuse is devilish. However, our Creator offers us the ability to forgive, be forgiven, and healing comes.

"...bearing with one another, and forgiving one another...even as Christ forgave you, so you must also do" (Colossians 3:13, NKJV).

That Newspaper on the Floor!

ANA BOUDET FORMAN

*Above all, love each other deeply,
because love covers over a multitude of sins.*

1 Peter 4:8, NIV

Why is it so hard for my husband to put the newspaper in the magazine basket next to his chair after he's finished reading it, instead of leaving it all over the floor?

It is like any typical afternoon driving my girls home from school. I'm trying to concentrate on the traffic, but my mind is going a mile a minute as I think about the errands I need to run before I go home. My older daughter needs fabric paint to decorate a T-shirt. It is my Kindergartener's turn to bring the snack. Oh, gosh…what's a healthy snack? Those young moms are always so clever with their homemade granola bars decorated with raisin smiley faces. I'm too old to have a five-year-old! What am I cooking tonight? Could my husband pick up dinner?

The cell phone rings and snaps me back out of my mental tirade. It's my husband who calmly informs me that after his routine blood work that morning his doctor called and told him he didn't like the numbers of his platelet count. He wants my husband to have another blood test immediately. Okay, I say, and wonder out loud what it all means. My husband shrugs off my question by telling me the doctor is just being overly cautious. We hang up, with my husband promising to be home soon with dinner. But I'm left with a knot in the pit of my stomach. This isn't a big deal, is it?

By 8 o'clock that evening we are at the hospital on the oncology floor waiting for more blood work results. As it has turned out, my husband's platelet counts are so low the second time around that his doctor wants him admitted to the hospital. I'm somewhere between numb and dazed as I hear words like leukemia and bone marrow biopsy. It will take several days for any conclusive diagnosis, so we just have to wait.

Each night during the time my husband was in the hospital, I tried to keep a normal routine. As I got ready for bed, I checked in on my five-year-old and adjusted her favorite teddy bear to fit cozily under her arm. I poked my head into my teenager's room and told her to get off the phone and go to sleep! I'd always give the family room a quick look and pick up any wayward pair of shoes and such.

Ordinarily, I'd dig out the remote from a seat cushion and routinely collect and put away the newspaper that my husband would have left on the floor. But on those nights the newspaper was already folded in the magazine basket. I had put it there earlier because I had not had time to read it, and of course, my husband wasn't home to read it either. I broke down in tears.

That night I knelt on my bedroom floor and prayed. My prayer wasn't particularly eloquent. I just prayed that God would bring my husband home so he would be able to toss that newspaper on the floor. A couple of days later, we received the results of the biopsy. It was not leukemia. His condition was brought on by medication and was easily treated.

The evening my husband came home from the hospital the house was filled with joyful commotion and family. Late that night, the house finally quiet, I followed my usual bedtime routine. I tidied up the sofa cushions, folded the afghan, and noticed the newspaper strewn on the floor next to my husband's chair. As I picked it up and placed it in the basket, my eyes swelled with tears. I had never been so happy to pick up a newspaper in my entire life.

Years have passed since that incident. I have picked up that newspaper many a night. I'm not going to pretend I'm giddy about having to do it every time, but has my attitude changed! I know it is a privilege to have people to love and care for… and to be loved and cared for in return. I'll never forget when there was no need to pick up that newspaper, and I thank God each night as I fold that paper and put it neatly back in the basket.

Sweet Words

PATTY KNITTEL

*"Dear friends, since God so loved us,
we also ought to love one another"*

1 John 4:11, NIV

My mother-in-law came to live with us for her last ten months of her life. She had chronic myeloid leukemia and had fought it for nine years.

I knew all along this was the right thing to do when the time came. But, I have to admit, I was apprehensive about having her with us all the time. I always felt I had disappointed her as a daughter-in-law because she had always looked forward to someone who liked feminine things, like cooking and sewing. Her tastes in decoration hadn't fit my taste, either, so when she asked us what we wanted before she sold everything, I only picked the grandfather clock, and her Franciscan dishes.

She moved up to Oregon from California and settled in. It was a huge move for her and yet she handled it so well. She had to have known she didn't have long to live, thus resigning herself to the move. The grandfather clock and dishware were among the few belongings she brought with her.

I was working part-time so it was nice to have her there to greet the kids when they came home from school. It was also great when she volunteered to cook supper sometimes. For the most part, though, she stayed to herself in her basement room complete with her own refrigerator and TV.

It actually came to the point that I was trying to get her to join us when we watched TV, when we had company, or when we went out to a movie. But she didn't want to intrude. I really felt bad about it. My husband tried to assure me she could be stubborn and not to take it personally.

As the months passed, her strength began to go down and she needed blood transfusions one or two times a week for energy. Oh, how she hated those. She was so frail but determined to keep fighting the disease. The medication was no longer effective. She was dying, but we didn't talk about it.

Finally, the doctor suggested hospice. She surprisingly agreed. She knew it would help us out, too, as we were taking turns helping her at night. A week into their care, the visiting nurse sat down with her to talk about the transfusions. She told mother she didn't have to have any more unless she wanted them. It was like giving her permission to let go. She stopped them that week.

A hospital bed was put in the living room. She was going downhill fast. She had a terrible fall one night as she tried to get to the bathroom without calling us to help.

A few nights later, I was tucking her into bed. I told her goodnight, and she said in a frail voice, "Goodnight, sweet thing." I was glad it was dark because the tears welled up in my eyes. I kissed her and went to my room. Those were her last words to me.

She died the next day. She left me with the gift of knowing she loved me. I will always cherish that. I hope I let my family know each day that I love them, not waiting for tragedy to wake me to the opportunity.

"Like apples of gold in settings of silver is a word spoken in right circumstances" (Proverbs 25:11, NASB).

Hearing by God's Grace

KIMBERLEY QUINNIE

> *"...Nothing in all creation will ever be able to separate us from the love of God..."*
> **Romans 8:39, NLT**

"Kimberly! Kimberly!" called my mother. "I love you, too!" I replied from another room in the house. The entire house erupted with laughter as my brothers held their sides and rolled on the floor. To my dismay, I had done it...again. Would it ever get better? Would I ever be able to understand the words people expressed when speaking to me at a distance? Would I always need to see a person's mouth when they spoke to me in order to understand them?

Being hearing impaired has never been easy. Sometimes, I'd try to shield myself from the taunts and cruelty of other children by making them laugh or being the quietest in the group because of the awkwardness of the hearing aids I wore. I obtained my first pair in 1985 when it wasn't really popular to be that kind of different. My siblings and mother helped me adjust to them by playing games and practicing "distance hearing" with me and teaching me to have self-confidence. They taught me to not be afraid to "try" to hear the things in my environment, encouraging me to be the best in everything that I attempted in life. The fact that everybody has something that is unique about them instilled in me a desire to help others that struggle with the same disability. My family told me that one day I would be a very influential person in the field of the hearing impaired.

As a child growing up in the '80s, I found it difficult to separate my personality from my disability. I was "the kid with the hearing aids" and it seemed as though my aids announced my presence everywhere I went. Children would stare and adults would whisper. It was so uncomfortable that I began to feel as though I was some sort of alien from outer space at times. It was *not* easy. My siblings encouraged me to explain to others that I was hearing impaired and that hearing aids helped me to hear more clearly. *I* simply wanted to live a life that didn't point to my ears so much.

I begged my mother to buy every new hearing aid that was invented in a smaller version than the one that I currently had. As I grew into my teenage years, I noticed that the difficulties that I experienced in school as a hearing-impaired individual began to define my life. Every school I attended was characterized by teachers that either helped or hurt me because of my disability. In college, some of my instructors created difficulties pertaining to my lack of ability to hearing things clearly. Every experience made me stronger in the face of adversity even when it hurt the very core of my being. My family always encouraged me to move forward because "God has a special work for you to do for the deaf and hard of hearing" and that I should use my disability for the advancement of others rather than allow it to be a hindrance for myself.

Because of the struggles I faced, the Lord placed within me a desire to help others with hearing disabilities. I attended a small university and majored in Deaf Education. This prepared me to face the world armed with the mentality that deaf and hard of hearing people can be successful, too! I created a deaf ministry, teaching groups of people to use sign language. I started sign language choirs in various locations as a ministry to the deaf. Many lives were touched, and the effects of my ministry are still felt in different parts of the world today. Since graduating from college, my profession has exposed me to undreamable advantages! I became a deaf advocate, teaching parents of hearing-impaired children how to communicate with their child. I also teach children to succeed academically despite their disability.

My ministry has touched the world in a very unique way, allowing my musical sign language ministry to be a blessing wherever I go. My life's motto has become: *nothing* can separate us from God's love, not even deafness!

I Love You Just the Way You Are!

DAWN S. BROWN

> *"But God showed his great love for us by sending Christ to die for us while we were still sinners."*
>
> **Romans 5:8, NLT**

One day my three-year-old son did something and I yelled at him. A few minutes later, as I realized I had completely over-reacted, I went back to him and told him Mommy was wrong for yelling and asked him for forgiveness. He took his little hands and cupped my face and replied, "That's okay, Mommy. I forgive you." And then he added sweetly, "I love you just the way you are!"

My heart melted! I had never heard him say that last part before, and the words permeated my heart, as they do even now, as I replay them again. They were the loving words a mom, who often feels like a failure, needed to hear.

Interestingly, ever since, I've come to believe that is exactly what God says about his love toward me, "I love you just the way you are. It doesn't matter what you've done, who you have hurt, or how bad a mess you've made of your life. I love you just the way you are!" In Romans 5, Paul writes of God's love for us while we were still in sin. You see, even before we realize our wrong, even before we come to God for forgiveness, he had already demonstrated his great love for us by dying on the cross for our sins. The chapter goes on to say we were "enemies of God" and yet his love was so great, so unconditional, so unchanging that even before you and I wanted anything to do with him, he loved us. That means God's love is not dependent on our goodness. He doesn't love us more because we're good and love us less because we're bad. His love is the kind of love that says in word and action, "I love you just the way you are!"

Once we understand that God's love for us is unconditional and non-changing, we ought to be like my toddler son, and graciously dispense that same kind of love to others. Whether we feel wronged by our spouse or a friend, exasperated by our kids, or perhaps a boss who is demanding, unreasonable, maybe even condescending– understanding God's great, unconditional love should compel us to love others, no matter how undeserving they may seem! Remember, they, too, were created in the image of God, and have intrinsic worth in his sight. The relationship may be strained, and we may not like everything about that person, but loving others like we are loved by God means we are quick to forgive and willing to work to restore the brokenness in every relationship.

Of course, there are still days when my son still tries my patience (as kids sometimes do) but now, I rest in God's unfailing love, and trust that his presence is with me and strengthening me with exactly what I need to rightly represent him and his amazing love. Loving our children and others just the way they are helps them understand that no matter what they say or do, God loves them just the way they are. If I sow that seed into their tender hearts, I trust that it will reap in them a genuine love for their Savior, too.

Each day, you and I get to practice demonstrating unconditional love. Some days are better than others, but as we keep our minds focused on Jesus, the greatest example of love the world has ever known, then we will increasingly become more loving.

What a difference we would see in the world around us if we could extend accepting, forgiving, and non-judgmental love to those we marry, work with, even those who live on our street. What peaceful places our homes, workplaces, and neighborhoods would be! Oh, that we would accept Jesus' love and love others just the way they are.

As you head out to the busy life that awaits you, consider this. Whether at home, at work, maybe in the car with the kids—others will disappoint you, mess up, overreact, and mistreat you! We do it, too. And God still loves us. God *still* loves us! Today, there will be opportunity for you to share God's unconditional, undeserving love with someone.

A Turnaround

ARLENE SALIBA

"Teach me, O Lord, the way of Your statutes, and I shall keep it to the end. Give me understanding and I shall keep Your law; indeed, I shall observe it with my whole heart."

Psalm 119:33-34, NKJV

"I'm sorry to bother you. I know you are here to do paperwork, but the wife of one of our patients wants to talk to you," the clinic nurse said. The day was reserved for reviewing lab results and notifying patients of those results. Spouses usually accompany the patient. If this woman had come by herself, there must be a real problem.

The nurse ushered in a distressed woman, who told me her husband was drinking six to eight beers every day, falling because of seizures, and was not contributing to the home chores or expenses. She was doing everything in the house including caring for their child with special needs and working outside the home. She didn't like seeing him have seizures and didn't understand why he was having them even if he had not missed his medications. He was not abusive verbally or physically. He just didn't DO anything but sit around and drink. She was tired and fed up but also worried about her husband. She asked for advice ... or the name of a lawyer I could recommend.

"Do you love him?" I asked. Through sobs and tears she nodded her head. A lawyer's name was not on my list that day. We talked about her role as a wife and mother.

I asked her to be the best wife she could possibly be no matter what her husband did and let the chips fall where they will. She was reminded to also care for herself. She did not have to be super woman and do everything.

A few days later, she was back with her husband who now had an appointment. The tension in the room was palpable. She sat in a corner with her arms folded. Weary eyes of steel stared at the wall. He was downcast, eyes slightly bloodshot and obviously nervous. He looked like a broken man–almost like a child who had been scolded and didn't know where to hide. He said, "This is a wake-up call and I don't know what to do. She handed me divorce papers yesterday. I don't want this. Please help me."

After making sure that he was physically intact, my advice to them was: "Take your medicines like you should. Eat nutritious food, not empty calories.

Stop buying beer. Be active. Go for a walk together . . . and hold hands. Reaffirm one another during this walk. This is not a time to argue or discuss issues. Enjoy each other's company. Go to church together. Pray together. Lastly, forgive one another."

"That's it?" he said. "I can do that. I'll eat whatever she puts in front of me. We live near the lake; we can walk there. I just don't know if she will hold my hand after all that I have done. I used to go to church with her until…" He looked nervously at her. She threw daggers at him with her eyes. He looked away then back at her hopefully. She smiled weakly and said "We can give it a try. I really don't want a divorce, but I'm not going to put up with you the way you were."

In a month they were back. From outside the examining room I could hear them talking and giggling like high school sweethearts. "This is the man I married!" she said. Her husband had not had any beer since leaving the clinic the month before. He also had not had any seizures. They were doing everything I suggested and more. He was working in the yard on projects that had been neglected. Their daughter was much happier also.

The divorce papers had been burned. They were working on a weight loss program together and planning a short vacation. They were thankful for a new direction in their lives. So was I.

God Says, "I Love You"

JOANNE CORTES

"But God is so rich in mercy, and he loved us so much."
Ephesians 2:4, NLT

The other day I was busy working and my son asked for something to eat, so I gave him a snack. Five minutes later he was thirsty. A few minutes after, "Mom, can I watch something, please?"

"Honey, I am trying to work here, go play." At that moment I began to get a little stressed.

"Mom, I'm hungry again,"

"Mom, can you fix this toy?"

"Mom, play with me."

By now I was more concerned about my work getting done than helping my child. I was overwhelmed by so many requests that I snapped at him, "Leave me alone! Can't you see I'm working? Go to your playroom."

Before he went sadly to his playroom, he said "I love you, Mom."

Hold on, did I hear right? Did my son just say that he loved me after the way I've been treating him? This made me feel really bad, like the worst mom ever. *What did I just do? He is my son. What is wrong with me? Nothing is more important than him!*

Have you felt this way before? Guilty of ignoring your child and snapping at him just because he asked? Maybe you don't have a child, but you may have treated someone unfairly because you were too busy. At times we get caught up in all of life's demanding activities, we are overwhelmed and stressed, causing us to mistreat and hurt people, especially those closest to us. We tell them to leave us alone, we don't have time, we don't call back, we don't spend time together, or sit around the table for dinner— we are just too busy. We isolate ourselves in our "to-do list" in this harsh world only to later realize that we are missing life's most valuable blessings, awesome quality time with our family and great relationships with our friends, neighbors, and colleagues.

The saddest thing is that at times I act this way with God. Just like my son wanted to spend time with me, God is next to me wanting to spend time together. He wants to share special moments and bless me with his presence, but I push him away.

And he still says: "I love you!" And he says those same words to you. These words are all we need to hear to break us and to help us realize he loves us. Though at times he may not be on our priority list, he patiently waits for us to say, "I love you, too! Let's spend some time together."

Life is too short to not spend time with the One person who loves us more than anyone or anything.

Take time today to talk with God. Throughout the day, tell him what you are going through. He sees and knows everything, yet he wants to hear it from you. He wants you to acknowledge his presence. He wants to bless you and love you more than you could ever imagine! He wants you to know that he is available 24/7 for you!

If you haven't yet done so, make a commitment to begin your day communicating with God and taking time to love your family and friends. When you do this, it will result in inner peace, greater happiness, better relationships, stronger faith, and true satisfaction for you and your loved ones. God will be happy, too.

And of course, when you are fulfilled and blessed, success in your work, inside and outside the home, will follow.

Heaven's Stand-In

COLLENE KELLY

"The Lord said, 'Go out and stand on the mountain in the presence of the Lord, for the Lord is about to pass by.'"

1 King 19:11, NIV

Although the late summer sun shone brightly, it did not warm my husband's heart.

"I don't know if I want to stay in the ministry. Nothing seems to change, and who really cares about whether the church fails or not? I'm still young. I can go back to school and do something different," he said.

It wasn't the first time he had verbalized these thoughts. In fact, over the previous several weeks, his courage for the incessant calling of ministry had been as low as the attendance at prayer meeting. And although I cared about my spouse, I couldn't relate to his restlessness.

Nodding and smiling at the members the next day, I settled, with our toddler, into a pew and prepared for an hour of church. Since I had heard the same sermon just seven days earlier at another of our churches, I knew I could coast through this week, the story of Elijah running from Jezebel still quite fresh in memory. But instead I began to wonder about the "Elijah" in my life. How could the shepherd of the flock feel so much like getting away from the sheepfold? Why couldn't he lie down in green pastures and drink from still water himself?

Sometimes something miraculous happens during a sermon. Surely that is part of the reason we are admonished not to forsake the assembling of ourselves together, and all the more so as Jesus' return nears (see Hebrews 10:25). Sometimes the Spirit plucks an arrow from the quiver of the Word and shoots it directly to the heart.

As my disgruntled thoughts jumbled about, I kept one ear to the sermon and pondered Elijah's story: *"…while he himself went a day's journey into the desert. He came to a broom tree, sat down under it and prayed that he might die. 'I have had enough, Lord,' he said. 'Take my life; I am no better than my ancestors.' Then he lay down under the tree and fell asleep. All at once an angel touched him and said, 'Get up and eat.' He looked around, and there by his head was a cake of bread baked over hot coals, and a jar of water. He ate and drank and then lay down again"* (1 Kings 19:4-6, NIV).

And then it was that the great Shepherd spoke to me: "When my servant ran away, I sent an angel to feed and care for him. What are you doing to care for your Elijah?" Chastened and chagrined, I repented of my hard heart, and accepted anew the ministry of encouragement. Challenges come and go. Opportunities and requests to serve are unending, but my greatest ministry potential is to care for my husband.

Every man who stands for Jesus faces moments when he feels alone. Satan whispers discouraging sentiments to weaken his faith, occasionally even through trusted friends or family. Plans will fail, and days are long. When labor is exhausting, friends misunderstand, and life seems only uphill, then it is that we can care as the angel did for Elijah.

We can listen, love, and encourage, give the gift of understanding, feel his pain, and bring him to Jesus in prayer. Elijah had no wife, and God sent him a heavenly messenger. Your husband has you–heaven's angel for the Elijah in your life.

And, as the continuation of Elijah's story whispers, we can remember that sometimes he needs time, as well as rest and refreshment, in order to regain his energy and courage so he can get back to the fray. *"The angel of the Lord came back a second time and touched him and said, 'Get up and eat, for the journey is too much for you.' So he got up and ate and drank. Strengthened by that food, he traveled forty days and forty nights until he reached Horeb, the mountain of God. There he went into a cave and spent the night. The next morning, the Lord instructed him, 'Go out and stand on the mountain in the presence of the Lord, for the Lord is about to pass by'"* (see 1 Kings 19:7-9, 11, NIV).

Then in quick succession came a mountain shattering wind, an earthquake, and a fire, followed by a still, small voice that would remind him that although in his discouragement, Elijah had decided that he alone was left to stand for God, there were still 7,000 faithful men in Israel. In this, Elijah found comfort, hope, and rejuvenation.

Trust the Expert

CARLA BAKER

"And the peace of God, which transcends all understanding, will guard your hearts and your minds in Christ Jesus."

Philippians 4:7, NIV

On a busy Sunday afternoon, I had just finished cleaning the kitchen after a late lunch. As I mentally planned my chores for the rest of the day, the back door burst open and in bounded my 12-year-old son, Brandon.

"Mom!" he said in a strange voice. When I turned to look at him, I first noticed that his face registered a look of alarm. Then I quickly saw the reason for his distress: blood was dripping from his hand and arm.

Though my instinctive reaction to the sight of blood is to panic and look away, I knew I had to stay calm and find out the nature of the injury. As I put his hand under the faucet to wash off the blood and get a look at the damage, I saw that the skin appeared to be torn away from the tip of his right index finger, leaving the bone exposed and jagged-looking.

With a quivering voice, Brandon gave me a sketchy description of what had happened. He had been riding his bicycle in the neighborhood when the chain came off the gears. Without stopping to get off the bike, he bent over to guide the chain back onto the gears as the wheels were turning. His right index finger got caught between the chain and gears, and the tip of the finger was mashed.

As calmly as I could, I wrapped a kitchen towel around his hand, and we headed to the hospital emergency room. When we were ushered into the examination cubicle, I was relieved to learn that the doctor examining Brandon's finger was a surgeon. He said that the bone was splintered and would not heal, so the splintered portion, just a few millimeters, had to be clipped off. He reassured us that the skin would soon grow back over the tip and Brandon would have full use of the finger again, although it would be quite sensitive for a while.

Brandon had always been a squeamish kid who couldn't stand the sight of blood, but I noticed that as the surgeon clipped away the splintered bone and sutured the skin back together, Brandon watched intently during the entire process. As we drove home, I asked why he had watched while the surgeon worked on his hand. It had been too gory for me. Brandon's reply astonished me: "I was afraid the doctor would decide to cut off my whole finger, and I wasn't going to let him."

I had to hide a rueful smile at the unfounded fears of a child–fears that only increased his agony during his emergency room experience. He would have had a much easier time had he trusted the person in charge, who was trained and knew exactly what to do.

Since that day I have reflected on the times that I, too, fail to experience peace of mind because I don't trust the One who has the answers to all my problems and is more than willing to help me.

The apostle Paul tells us in Philippians 4:6-7 how to experience peace of mind in even the most trying circumstances: *"Do not be anxious about anything, but in every situation, by prayer and petition, with thanksgiving, present your requests to God. And the peace of God, which transcends all understanding, will guard your hearts and your minds in Christ Jesus"* (NIV).

How reassuring to know that our heavenly Father not only has the answers to all our questions and problems, but he always wants the very best for his children.

He must shake his head in amazement when we fail to take advantage of the peace that comes from trusting in his tender care.

Lord, please give me faith to trust you more.

Too Busy to Rest

CHERYL MOSELEY

"...Come with me by yourselves to a quiet place and get some rest."
Mark 6:31, NIV

Scanning quickly through her planner, Sarah knew she had another busy week ahead. Every day was full of activities and this week she had agreed to work overtime. Apart from going to work and taking the children to their various after-school programs, Sarah needed to go to the gym, attend meetings, arrange a car service, do the grocery shopping and housework, and continue with her online Spanish course. Even for Sarah it looked like a hectic week.

In fact, most weeks were the same. Life was so busy that Sarah had little time for relaxation and leisure. She often spent half the night catching up on chores and was always up early the next day after only a few hours' sleep. Sarah was a young, working mom with lots of energy;

she enjoyed her busy lifestyle, but lately she was beginning to feel tired. She tried to shake off the feeling and carry on, telling herself how important her tasks were.

On Monday morning after dropping the children at school, Sarah rushed to the gym for a half-hour exercise class. After that it was on to work. Her boss was taking assessments of his staff that afternoon, so everyone in the office was under pressure to perform. One thing after another seemed to go wrong that morning and by lunch time Sarah felt extremely stressed and anxious. There was still so much to do she didn't have time for a break, so she worked through lunch. Often Sarah would wish she could just sit down and do nothing for five minutes, but it never happened!

Around five o'clock Sarah put the finishing touches to an important presentation for a client, which needed to be mailed out that day. As she was rushing downstairs to the mail room she suddenly felt faint and the room began to spin. Then everything went black. She woke feeling pain in her right leg. Looking around she realized she was in the hospital, her leg in plaster. She had blacked out on the stairs and taken a fall. The doctor stood by her bed.

"You had a nasty fall" he told her. "It's going to take many weeks and lots of rest for your leg to heal."

Great! How could she afford to rest? There was so much to do. At first Sarah felt this was a nightmare situation. How would everything get done? Who would take the kids to school? What would happen to her job? Thoughts like this crowded her mind until she remembered something her mother taught her as a child. It was a verse from the Bible: *"Come to me all you who are weary and burdened, and I will give you rest. Take my yoke upon you and learn from me for I am gentle and humble in heart, and you will find rest for your souls"* (Matthew 11:28-29, NIV).

It was then she realized that God was using these circumstances to enable her to get the rest she so desired and needed, rest her body had been crying out for.

Sarah's leg healed and she returned to work. Today she lives a much more balanced lifestyle. She makes time to rest every day—a walk in the park, reading a good book, or maybe just closing her eyes and putting her feet up. She even makes sure she gets a good night's sleep, too. Life has changed a lot for Sarah, but the funny thing is, she says she achieves so much more now than she ever did before!

My Friend's Baditude

CODI JAHN

"Rejoice always; pray without ceasing; in everything give thanks; for this is God's will for you in Christ Jesus."

1 Thessalonians 5:15, 18, NASB

Attitude is everything. We've all heard it. But can you really control your attitude in all circumstances? A friend of mine told a story years ago about attitude that I've never forgotten. This friend was diagnosed with an aggressive form of cancer that would require intense therapy if he was going to have any shot at all of beating it. He and his wife both quit their jobs and relocated cross country to be near the treatment facility. The treatments were exhausting and incredibly painful.

One day, not unlike all the others during his treatment, my friend was riding the elevator up to the cancer treatment floor. Another gentleman stepped on and they began riding up together.

"Beautiful day outside, isn't it?" commented the passenger, enthusiastically. My friend glanced up at him and his cheery demeanor. He hadn't really noticed the weather; he was a little preoccupied trying to beat cancer! But then what would this guy know of that?

In his world, thought my friend, *there's nothing more important to focus your energy on than the weather. He has no idea what it is like to look death in the face every day and try to find the strength to struggle on.* They continued riding up, both eventually stopping at the cancer floor.

My friend waited patiently to sign in behind Mr. Optimistic. After all, anyone going through what he was going through could use a visitor like him. As he removed his jacket and hat, my friend saw his hairless head and realized he was no visitor; he, too, was there for the fight of his life. He was a fellow cancer patient, no different than my friend, yet he had chosen to see beauty despite all the ugliness he was up against.

My friend never saw him again. They never rode the elevator up together after that, but he learned an important lesson that day that he later shared with me. No matter what your circumstance, or what battles you're fighting, you control your attitude. Life may dictate your surroundings and those around you may control your decisions, but only you determine your attitude.

I was surprised to hear this story from my friend, someone I had always considered to personify optimism. Yet even he was susceptible to life's pressures. He seemed embarrassed as he shared his experience, but he had learned a valuable lesson about his attitude.

I have never battled cancer or fought for my life. To be honest, things have been pretty easy. Still, each day presents new obstacles. As a newly transitioned stay-at-home mom, I've seen more lately than usual. During one of my son's notorious temper tantrums, I began sinking into despair, remembering the "good times" I'd had at my fulfilling job and all the adult interaction it entailed (something I get very little of now). I felt sorry for myself and wondered why I had ever wanted to do this in the first place.

Just then I thought of my friend and his experience with a stranger on an elevator. I, too, was choosing my own attitude. Staying home with my son had been a dream of mine for years, so was I going to let a tantrum or two really impair my attitude? How would that help my son's struggling attitude?

Instead of feeling sorry for myself, I began to feel thankful for the opportunity before me: being able to influence and touch my children's lives in a way I had always wished to . . . and having enough time to do it.

Fear Not the Cat

JEAN THOMASON ("MISS PATTY CAKE")

"The Lord is my shepherd, I lack nothing.…
He guides me along the right paths for his name's sake."

Psalm 23:1, 3, NIV

It was nearly noon and the trip to the grocery store had taken longer than I wanted. All three of us were cranky. Grocery shopping takes more energy than I ever think it will. And, it really wears out the children! I finally checked out, wrestled them into the car, and drove toward home.

"Mommy, I'm hungry. I'm thirsty, too. How long till we get home? Will it rain today? What color is the moon? Do fish have teeth? Christopher won't be quiet!"

Even getting out of the car was a chore! My ten-month-old son was fussing loudly and was heavy on my right arm in the car carrier while my other arm was loaded with grocery bags. "Go straight into the house please," I instructed twenty-seven-month-old

Marilyn, who slowly walked up the front porch stairs in front of me. I felt like a shepherd, herding her toward the door. Time for lunch and naps. "Please hurry! Mommy is *tired*."

Suddenly she stopped, screamed, and ran to the other end of our wide front porch. There was a kitty near our front door. Not our kitty–a strange kitty–a big, hairy cat. Marilyn was terrified! Speaking soothing words to Marilyn, I walked calmly past the cat to the door. It looked at me.

I looked at it. It didn't move. I unlocked the front door, being careful not to drop bags or baby. "Come on sweetie, mommy sees the cat," I urged. "The cat won't get you." I shooed the cat. It lazily walked a few feet from the door. Marilyn was not moving. "Honey, I won't let the cat hurt you."

"The cat, the cat!" she wailed. Holding the door open, I said, "The kitty will not hurt you. Just please run on into the house."

"No. No! It's a *big* cat!" she whined. Frustrated, I said, "Marilyn, look at me.

Don't look at the cat. Walk to *me* and come into the house." She didn't move. (My arms are aching now).

"Please honey–don't look at the cat," I said. "I will not let the cat hurt you. Look at me." I was begging...rather *loudly* now–the baby was crying and I was on the brink....

"Sweetie! If that cat comes anywhere near you, I will KICK it away!"

Finally! After much coaxing she took a tentative step, looked at me, then the cat, then me, the cat, me, cat, and *ran* past me into the house. Whew! I turned to the cat, stomped my foot and said, "Scat!" The strange cat flew off our porch, never to return.

Later, I pondered that episode, and had an "AHA" moment. How like our Father to show me something profound in a typical "mothering" day. From his perspective, I am that scared little girl–afraid of the "cats" in my life. The Father is urging me, "look at *Me*–not the cats. Keep your eyes on me–I will not let the 'cats' hurt you. Walk the way. I will show you. I am a good shepherd, herding you to a safe place. I have set before you an open door. Trust *Me*, rely on *Me*."

Wow! I have found "mothering" to be the place where I learn the most about God's "Fathering."

Today, in your mothering, ask the Father to show you how your parenting can reflect his parenting. He is able to *kick that scary cat* off your porch!

"*The Lord is my shepherd, I lack nothing.… He guides me along the right paths for his name's sake. Even though I walk through the valley of the shadow of 'CATS' I will fear no evil, for you are with me….*" (Psalm 23:1-4, NIV, excerpted–my own rendition, of course!)

Just a Routine Test

PATRICIA BODI

> *"Inasmuch as ye have done it unto one of the least of these my brethren, ye have done it unto me."*
>
> **Matthew 25:40, KJV**

The postcard came from the doctor's office reminding me it was time for the annual checkup. It was in January and, unfortunately, I was knee-deep in taxes. You see—I'm an accountant-tax-preparer. I just didn't have time for doctor's visits. So I neglected to call for an appointment.

Once the filing period was over and I had returned from a week's vacation with my mother in Florida, I went in to see the physician on April 30. About ten days later I received a phone call at my home from my doctor's office informing me that I had abnormal cells and they had made an appointment with a specialist for a biopsy.

After I had allowed this information to soak in and I had talked privately with the Lord about it, I realized I needed to talk further about it. But who would I call? Should I call a family member? After all, I had a mother and four sisters living in the area. Should I call a classmate from academy days or college? Should I call one of my children? No, I called a good friend from church, Betty.

First, Betty and I just talked. Then she prayed a beautiful prayer with me over the telephone as she often does with church friends.

Finally, Betty insisted on going with me to the physician's office the next week. I've been single for many years and am not used to being accompanied to the doctor's office. However, Betty was so persuasive that I easily acquiesced. If you knew Betty, you would have no problem hearing her say, "We'll have lunch after the biopsy." And we did. Afterwards I went in to work.

And then I waited and waited for the verdict. Now if you have ever had a biopsy, you know it takes FOREVER to learn the results! After the results–"inconclusive"–I returned to the doctor's office. Then I was instructed to use a topical application for about a month. During this time my father was in hospice on his deathbed, so I cancelled my return visit. After my dad's funeral, I returned to the doctor's office for the next test.

One week later, my doctor's office called me at work to arrange for laser surgery. Unfortunately, the treatment had made no difference.

The surgery took place at the local hospital where I had been a volunteer chaplain assistant for ten years. One month later, I was happy to learn the lab results showed it was precancerous and "the margins are clear."

Praise the Lord!

When I was most in need of emotional and spiritual support, Betty was there to provide nurturing to a church sister. Now, isn't that what God talks about in Matthew 25:40? *"Inasmuch as ye have done it unto one of the least of these my brethren, ye have done it unto me"* (KJV).

It's been suggested that how we treat others is literally how we're treating our Savior. If we could always remember him, we would see each other through his eyes. We'd be more forgiving, more compassionate, and more giving. We'd reach out to others, lift, build and bless, for in doing so, we know we're doing what God expects of his church. Furthermore, we would be following the example of my good friend, Betty.

"Therefore encourage one another and build each other up, just as in fact you are doing" (1 Thessalonians 5:11, NIV).

Angels All Around Us!

JUDITH NEWTON

"Don't forget to show hospitality to strangers, for some who have done this have entertained angels without realizing it!"

Hebrews 13:2, NLT

My husband and I were on a vacation in Oahu, Hawaii. It was our anniversary and we were having a fantastic time. Now before I go further, I have to tell you how awesome our God is. Before I left, one of my best friends came to me and told me that she felt the Lord was telling her to seriously pray for me while I was gone. She felt that I would be in some kind of danger. I just tucked her words in the back of my mind.

So we were on this beautiful island enjoying ourselves. We rented a car to take a tour of the island. At the car rental place the attendant warned us about the "south side" of the island. He said the currents were bad there, and sometimes rogue waves were known to carry people out to sea and they drowned. We both thanked him and drove away. I wasn't concerned much. I couldn't swim and I had no intention of getting that close to the ocean. When I was young I had almost drowned in a lake and I have been somewhat fearful of being in the water since then.

We were driving along admiring the cobalt blue skies, the lush green forests, and majestic vistas. We both felt like it was just a little bit of heaven. When we arrived at the south side, the view was absolutely spectacular, and we could see why people would want to walk the beach.

We decided to get out of the car and walk on the beach, back far enough we felt we were safe from any rogue wave. We walked along like a newly married couple, holding hands (even after thirty-two years of marriage, we still hold hands).

I wasn't concerned at all. I was sure we were far enough from the edge of the ocean to be safe. But suddenly, without any warning, a rogue wave dashed against the beach and immediately pulled us out to sea! I found myself being drawn down under the thrashing waves. I remember thinking, *I am going to die.* In my heart I cried out to the Lord.

I was being tumbled over and over against the coral reef there. I was being pushed deeper and deeper into the depths of the ocean and being buffeted by the pounding waves. I could feel the pull of the current on my body. I was being pummeled by the waves. I was choking on the sea water and everything seemed hopeless.

Suddenly I had the sensation of being gently plucked out of the water. The next thing I knew I was sitting on a log at the edge of the beach. People were all around me. They had seen we were in serious trouble and ran to see if they could help. Strangely, I was filled with a profound feeling of peace and calmness. My husband, who can swim well, was sitting on the beach close to me looking like a drowned cat.

I looked at my legs and feet and realized I had deep cuts all over them from the coral. I could tell one big toe was broken. My hands had cuts all over them as I had tried frantically to grab hold of something to help me. My right arm was sprained, and I was bruised all over. Yet, here I sat, perfectly calm and relaxed.

I should have been absolutely beside myself with fear and shock. But I wasn't! You see I KNEW that the Lord had an angel scoop me up out of the water and put me on that log. There was no other explanation for what happened.

Do angels exist? Oh yes, they certainly do.

As we travel through this world we are under the constant care and protection of heavenly angels. We all have a guardian angel that walks with us and guards us. So, I think we should be saying "thank you" daily to them for our care.

Taking the Plunge

ALICIA BRUXVOORT

"'Yes, come,' Jesus said. So Peter went over the side of the boat and walked on the water toward Jesus."

Matthew 14:29-30, NLT

We celebrated my daughter, Lizzy's, tenth birthday with a splash. Lathered in sunscreen and laden with beach towels, we hauled a minivan full of kids to a nearby water park for a poolside party. While the aquatic complex housed snaky waterslides, a walloping wave pool and a sprinkler-studded playground, the highlight of the day loomed four-stories high at the top of a tall timber tower. Though "The Rage" looked as daunting as its name, a steady thread of dripping adventurers wound like a colorful party streamer up the steep wooden stairs. At the pinnacle, bold blue signs invited riders to plummet down a two-hundred-foot drop to a small pool at the slide's end.

One by one, my daughter's party guests accepted the spine-tingling challenge. After flinging themselves down the fast and furious fall, they stormed the sundeck where I was enjoying a rare moment of relaxation. And they begged me to join them.

"Please, Mom," my birthday girl pleaded.

"Come with us this time." I glanced at the sky-high attraction, then at my daughter's hopeful face. Reluctantly, I slipped off my flip flops and headed for "The Rage." Moments later, I stood at the top of the infamous slide and looked down. My stomach flip-flopped as I watched my daughter and her friends speed to the shallow finish. Finally, I was the only one left on the wooden platform.

"Just lie on your back and give yourself a push," the lifeguard instructed as she smacked bubble gum and tediously twirled a silver whistle around her pointer finger. I could see my daughter jumping and clapping at the bottom of the ride as she anticipated my rookie run.

I stepped into the swirling water. *I was enjoying the party from my lawn chair,* I thought. Tentatively, I sat down at the top of the slide. *The water is freezing!* The drop looked daunting from my perspective. One push and I would drop two hundred feet. *Oh, the things we do for our kids.* I took a deep breath (and held it all the way to the bottom), reclined in the cold water, then grabbed the side of the slide. I closed my eyes and pushed my trembling body over the edge.

Water spewed into the air. My heart jumped to my throat. My backside momentarily lifted off the slide and then battered the side wall with a *thump*.

Adrenaline rushed. Lizzy screamed with delight. My bulleting body came to a splashing halt.

"You did it, Mom!" Lizzy applauded. "Wasn't that *awesome*?"

As I headed up the steps to do it all over again, I decided that the waterslide was an apt picture of my life with Jesus. Following him is an amazing ride, but sometimes the hardest part is simply taking *the plunge* of obedience.

"I want you and your family to move."

"Are you kidding, Lord? I'm happy right here in my lawn chair. See? I have friends, a great church, a thriving ministry…"

"I want you to surrender your career plans to me."

"But, Lord, I want to pursue *these* dreams."

"It's time to give your husband the reins. I created him to be the head of your family. Get out of the way and let him become the man I've created him to be."

"But, Lord, he's too busy to lead well. And he doesn't have the vision I do, and …."

And for every argument I have, the Author of this adventure called life urges, "Just take the plunge!"

Hesitantly I push my wary heart over the edge of my comfort zone, and hear my Savior cheer and holler, "Wasn't that an *awesome* ride? How did you like those splashes of joy? Didn't you love that adrenaline-pumping rush of dependency on ME? Did you feel your heart lift off the ground and soar?"

As I reach the end of my challenge, I can almost hear Jesus say, "Come on! Let's do it again!"

Really Lord, Her?

CODI JAHN

*"And you also are among those. . . who are called
To belong to Jesus Christ."*

Romans 1:6, NIV

This was a first. I had never met a "working girl" in person before. She wasn't nearly as glamorous or beautiful as Julia Roberts had been in "Pretty Woman." She was dirty and sloppily dressed. I could smell the lingering scent of cigarettes and alcohol permeating around her like a cloud. Her hands and face looked weathered. I tried not to stare as I walked by her, but I couldn't help myself. What was someone like *her* doing in our office building? I did my best to smile at her, but it was halfhearted. I quickly moved past her and sat down at my desk, hoping she would be gone in a few minutes. Soon my wish was granted and she was out the door.

After she was gone, I asked my boss about her. As it turned out she had stopped in briefly to visit him as he was a friend of a friend and she didn't know many people in the area. He didn't seem surprised by the visit or her condition. In his mind she was no different from anyone else. Was I the only one uncomfortable having a "working girl" hang out at our office?

She *was* different from us. Way different. According to my boss, her children had been taken by social services. She had spent years in prison on drug charges. This was all part of a world I couldn't relate to. I sat down at my desk again, unsure why no one else was concerned with this.

Suddenly it hit me. I felt ashamed as I thought back on the past several minutes. I thought about the parallel. No wonder they hated Jesus. They couldn't understand him. The faithful churchgoers, the Pharisees and Sadducees, must have been blown away by Jesus' willingness to surround himself so closely with people like *her*. I had always thought of the leaders in Jesus day as stuck in religious rut and unwilling to see what was right in front of them, and yet in looking at it, I wasn't so sure I would have been much different.

Jesus challenged norms. He broke tradition. He didn't care what others thought. He viewed all humanity in the same light. He dined with prostitutes, stayed with crooked tax collectors, and hung out with the illiterate. He would have been friends with *her*.

I was a good person! I had attended church regularly my whole life! I donated my time. I donated my money. I loved my neighbor... or did I? I thought about the scowl that had suddenly formed on my face when I saw *her*. Then I thought about what it would be like to have her over to my house for dinner.

Weird. As I pictured the scene in my mind, she didn't fit. I imagined awkward silences as we wouldn't have anything in common. It became easy to see how the religious leaders would have been uncomfortable around Jesus' friends. Forget that they were from a lower caste, maybe outcasts, yet in Jesus' mind they all fit under the same one-word description: redeemable. It didn't matter if they were dirty and homeless or religious and wealthy; in his mind, they were redeemable.

I was embarrassed. I had acted so poorly. I claimed to be a Christian and yet when someone didn't fit the mold I expected, I had turned my nose up at them. I learned an important lesson that day, both from our visitor and my non-church going boss who had been a friend to her when I certainly wasn't interested.

"If you love only those who love you, what reward is there for that? Even corrupt tax collectors do that much. If you are kind only to your friends, how are you different from anyone else? Even pagans do that. But you are to be perfect, even as your Father in heaven is perfect" (Matt. 5:46-48, NLT, selected).

I Got You, Girl!

DOROTHY DAVIS

*"Even when I walk through the darkest valley,
I will not be afraid, for you are close beside me."*

Psalm 23:4, NLT

I was excited and giddy about my get-away weekend with my husband. I had made reservations to stay at Yarrow Resort in Michigan. We planned to stay in a cabin, and I had made arrangements to have a picnic in the wooded area behind the golf course. I had contacted a close friend to make sure that DJ, our grandson, would be taken care of for worship and dinner.

We decided to leave at 3:00 AM to avoid traffic delays on I-94. I had packed a picnic basket with all of our favorite snacks, sparkling grape juice, and long-stemmed flutes. I had packed my husband's clothes for the trip so there would be one less thing for him to think about.

Before leaving I asked my husband, JD, to leave his cell phone at home because I didn't want any interruptions with our time of renewal. He won the debate by stating we needed to have a means of connecting with DJ if something were to happen while we were away.

I was driving and my husband was relaxing in his seat as we started down the highway. I looked over at him, and as I was checking the mirrors to make sure of the position of the other cars, I heard a loud explosion. My car spun around in the middle of the highway, smashed into the concrete median, and did another 360 and stopped on exit ramp 12. It felt as though I was at the State Fair riding in a bumper car. I could hardly breathe; my airbag had deployed and had literally knocked my breath out of me. I kept asking, "What happened?" By this time JD was fully awake and wanted to know if I was all right.

He freed himself from his deployed airbag and opened the door, so he could help me get out of the car. He wanted to know where I was hurt and what had just happened.

My response was, "I don't know." A car pulled up behind us and the young couple checked with us to make sure we weren't severely injured. They saw what had happened and they couldn't believe that we were able to walk away from the accident. A driver in a silver car had sped past them going at 90 miles per hour and had rammed into the rear of our car, then continued going down the highway. Chelsey, the young lady, asked if she could pray with me while we waited for the medics to come.

She began by saying, "Sovereign God, have mercy on this couple, may their lives be precious in your sight." I believe the angel that has been assigned to me was present with me during that accident. They stayed until the police arrived and gave their eyewitness testimony. The police thought I had fallen asleep at the wheel and the accident was my fault. I thank God that he allowed the angels to remain with us and to be our witnesses.

Fortunately, JD did not sustain any visible injuries. I, on the other hand, snapped my collarbone in two places. I was given a sling and medication to help me get through the healing process. JD was able to call an elder from our local church to come to the hospital and give us a ride home. I thank God that there are those who were willing to help in our time of emergency.

After looking at the pictures of our totaled car, I realized that had DJ gone with us, he would have sustained life-threatening injuries because the rear seat was now smashed into our front seats. Our God is an awesome God. We truly passed through the valley of death, but we had no fear because God whispered, "I got you, girl."

Act As If

SARA ALSUP

> *"You have persevered and have endured hardships for my name, and have not grown weary. Yet I hold this against you: You have forsaken the love you had at first. Consider how far you have fallen! Repent and do the things you did at first…"*
>
> **Revelation 3:2-5, NIV**

I was waiting for the left turn arrow early one morning, when I saw it. And I've never seen it again. It was like a "sign" for me. The license tag on the car in front of me said, "ACT AS IF." When I first read it, I was startled with the simple phrase. The more I sat in the line of waiting traffic, the more I puzzled over what the words could possibly mean.

My first inclination was to respond to myself, "What's the point?" I was in such a sleepy state of mind that morning that I wasn't in the mood to think deeply. I just wanted for the green arrow to appear in a hurry and to safely get to work. The longer the light stayed red, the more I couldn't help myself; I mused over and over the phrase, "Act as if."

Then I began to answer the license tag with the first things that popped into my head, like, "Act as if I really believe in God's love; act as if I really trust him; act as if I have great faith; act as if I truly love others."

These lightning quick ideas and themes shocked me! Here I am a Bible teacher telling my students how faithful God is. Now on a Wednesday morning at 7:00 AM I'm trying to convince myself. "What was I thinking? Where were my faith and my trust in the love of God? Where was my thankfulness? Why was I allowing my morning circumstances to dictate how I act and feel?" At that moment I was ashamed of my own selfishness and blindness to God.

In the time it took for the red light to change green, these thoughts flew through my mind. I was more perplexed than ever and could hardly keep my mind on work. During break I shared the mystery with the other gals in my office. As I did so, there was complete silence, no response. Their silence bewildered me. So I repeated the concise license message to them, but I was silently asking, "Was the message only for me and for me to discover the true meaning?"

At the point of hush, a new employee timidly raised her hand and began to explain that her life recently took an unexpected turn. Now this young gal was viewed as shy and perhaps a little standoffish. She began to tell us her very own personal dilemma.

With tiny tears threatening to roll from her round brown eyes, she acknowledged that she believed God was still in control of her very life and he still loved her—regardless of her personal suffering. None of us had any inkling of the secret pain she endured. "Why is this?" I asked myself. The clear answer was that she had been *acting as if* God was walking with her, sometimes carrying her along the daily path of life.

She got it! Her outlook showed she understood God's love and care, and her life showed only his grace.

Because of her personal outlook on God's grace for her, I felt the emotion of being ashamed of my own fragment of faith.

From this moment and during the day, I reflected on how many times and ways God had showed me his love and grace. Early that morning he had told me to "Get up." The next communication was when I saw the rectangular license plate message. The third message was the sweet voice of my coworker.

How could I doubt for one minute God's love and care for my life? How could I challenge his unfailing love?

Renewed with the blessed encouragements that God had sent to me, I picked myself up and put a thankful smile on my face and into my heart and moved on with considerable faith, trust, and love. My outlook was changed in moments of meaningful messages from the One who loves me most.

"You have persevered and have endured hardships for my name, and have not grown weary. Yet I hold this against you: You have forsaken the love you had at first. Consider how far you have fallen! Repent and do the things you did at first..." (Rev. 3:2-5, NIV).

Are You Afraid?

JOANNE CORTES

"For I am the LORD your God who takes hold of your right hand and says to you, do not fear; I will help you."

Isaiah 41:13, NIV

"Jesus loves me this I know, for the Bible tells me so. Little ones to him belong, they are weak but he is strong. Yes, Jesus loves me. Yes, Jesus loves me. Yes, Jesus loves me. The Bible tells me so."

I remember as a child, there were times I would wake up in the middle of the night, scared, fearful, because of a bad dream. It was hard going back to sleep after dreaming that a big monster was chasing me. I would toss and turn, asking God to catch that big monster and throw him far, far away so he would not bother me again, so I could sleep through the night. Every time I felt afraid, I would sing "Jesus loves me, this I know." I would sing it over and over, until I eventually fell asleep.

Singing this song always brought me peace. I knew that whenever that imaginary big monster would come to bother me, Jesus, who loved me, was stronger and bigger, and I felt safe knowing that I belonged to him and no monster, no matter how big and scary, could harm me. Even now, when at times I might be anxious, or afraid, I sing this song and it gives me the assurance that everything is going to be okay, because I know, Jesus loves me!

Last night, I woke up to the cries of my son Jose. I ran to his room and asked him what was happening. Half asleep, he started talking to me about flying mushrooms and turtles that were chasing him. He was afraid they were going to catch him. All he kept saying was "Mama, they are going to get me, they are going to get me." I realized he was having a bad dream and was taken back to my childhood days. I assured him that everything would be ok and began to sing "Jesus loves me this I know." When I finished the song, he requested that I sing it again and again. I sang until he peacefully dozed off, affirming once more that singing to Jesus when you are afraid and during times of distress, brings peace and helps to overcome fear.

Is there something that you're afraid of? Are you anxious about tomorrow? Is there a "monster," something that is keeping you far from your lifetime dreams and aspirations? Is there someone who is hurting you? Do you have fears that won't let you sleep?

Remember, Jesus loves you! He does not want you to be afraid or anxious. He has promised that he will be with you always and will give you the strength and courage to face any "monster" that may come your way.

God promises to hold your hand through any of life's circumstances. He says, "Do not fear, I am with you." He was with David when facing Goliath; with the three Hebrew boys in the fiery furnace; with Daniel in the lions' den; with Esther when she had to go before the king; with Mary, a virgin who was chosen to carry the Son of God; with the disciples on the boat in the midst of a storm. And he is with you today.

Next time flying mushrooms, turtles, or monsters of life chase after you and you don't know what to do or say, remember that you are not alone, and don't forget to sing, "Yes, Jesus loves me."

Prayer: Lord, you know my fears and anxieties. Please help me to trust in you. I know you will rescue and deliver me from any "monster."

Craft Night

JENNI GLASS

*There are 'friends' who destroy each other,
but a real friend sticks closer than a brother."*

Proverbs 18:24, NLT

As I pulled into my driveway, a wave of anxiety fell over me. I suddenly had a feeling that I had to be somewhere but had forgotten when and where. As someone who lives by a calendar would do, I panicked. I was certain that I had double checked my calendar earlier in the day as I thought about what I was going to do when I got home that evening. I checked my calendar on my phone and sure enough, there was nothing listed.

So why did I have this feeling that I was supposed to be somewhere? Then it hit me. It was Tuesday. That is when the tears started to stream down my face and memories flooded to my mind. Tuesday was "Craft Night." For me, Tuesday will always be craft night.

Best I can remember it started when my friend Tara and I were talking one day and she asked if I would like to come over for dinner on Tuesday night while her husband was at orchestra practice. Without hesitation I said "yes." I learned early on in our friendship that I should never turn down a meal at Tara's house. She is an amazing cook, and as a single female I hated to cook for one. Plus she always sent me home with lunch for the next day. She also mentioned to me about bringing over some crocheting or knitting to work on after dinner. Thus began a wonderful tradition of Craft Night.

Craft Night went on for many years. Periodically others would join us, but more often than not, it was just Tara and me. I learned to knit and improved my crocheting skills over the years. I even learned to sew, yet to this day my mom still doesn't believe that I know how to use a sewing machine. We talked a lot during these nights. Some nights were lighthearted and others were filled with tears as we discussed our jobs, families, friends, likes, dislikes, the future, and the list goes on. No topic was off limits.

In my mind, Craft Night would always exist. I couldn't imagine life without Craft Night. Then the news came. Tara told me that her husband had accepted a new job and they were moving to California. My heart sunk. My best friend was going to move 1,800 miles away. Even though I knew this was in God's plan, I was still sad.

That night in the driveway I realized that although we didn't live close to each other anymore, Craft Night would continue in my heart and mind. I also realized how blessed I was to have those many years of Craft Night to form such a strong bond with a friend. I don't have a sister, but I believe God blessed me with a sister named Tara.

Shortly after that night in my driveway, Tara and I were chatting via Web cam. I began to chuckle as I realized she was cooking and I was sewing as we talked, our first Virtual Craft Night. I made my first trip out to California about three months after Tara moved. For old time's sake, we set one night aside for Craft Night. As I sat at the sewing machine and Tara knitted a hat, my heart leaped for joy that Craft Night would always be a part of my life.

Epilogue: A few years have passed since Tara moved to California. I have learned in these past few years that some projects just require two people. During my last trip to California we worked on a purse project together that we started before she moved. I just can't bring myself to finish the project without her. So the project sits in my craft room waiting for Tara to come to Kansas City for a visit. Maybe I will actually get to use the purse next time I fly out to California.

The Gift of Trust

EVE RUSK

"But those who hope in the Lord will renew their strength. They will soar on wings like eagles; they will run and not grow weary, they will walk and not be faint."

Isaiah 40:31, NIV

It was already an extraordinary Thanksgiving weekend. My husband and I had traveled from Idaho to Arizona and Southern California to finalize his father's estate. Thanksgiving dinner was in a restaurant. While the food was good, the atmosphere just didn't resonate. It certainly wasn't home. Still, we were thankful to have something, since the friends we were staying with that evening already had other plans.

We arrived home after a long drive to find a voicemail message and a letter from the mammography center I had visited just ten days before for my annual screening. The letter said that something had been discovered that required further diagnostic tests and to please call and make an appointment. When I called, the receptionist was very encouraging, saying that 80 percent of these findings turn out to be nothing. I knew, though, that this was not "nothing."

"It looks suspicious, so we want to do a biopsy." Somewhere deep in me, those words caused terror. But outwardly, I was calm. My biopsy was scheduled for a Friday afternoon. The following Sunday was my husband's office Christmas party. It was surreal, being there in festive dress, surrounded by coworkers and their families, singing Christmas carols, eating delicious food. Outwardly, I was calm and trusting. Inside, my mind was racing. *It's probably cancer. How can I get this taken care of and still take care of my family, especially my granddaughter, who lives with us? How bad is it going to be?*

The radiologist told me he would have the results by Tuesday evening. So when the phone rang at 9 AM Tuesday, I was unprepared. Yes, it was cancer. But it was small and didn't appear to have spread.

Then the whirlwind started. Set up blood work and chest X-ray and surgical consultation. "You're so young—only forty-nine," I heard many times. Did I have any questions? I could only think of a few. I was still outwardly calm, but inside, my mind was racing again. That night, I wasn't feeling well, so I took my blood pressure:

190 over 110. Definitely not healthy. My fear that night wasn't about the cancer, but about having a stroke. I prayed to God that he would keep me alive and calm me. I was no longer outwardly calm.

My blood pressure lowered some the next day, but I went to see a doctor about it. I was an emotional mess. This wasn't the only stressful thing in my life that year. Of the major stress events, we had experienced several within a six-month period. The doctor recognized the load I was carrying and gave me something to help. It allowed my mind to slow down, to recognize that I needed help from others, and from God.

Two days before Christmas, I had a lumpectomy. I wasn't calm—I was scared. I knew God would be with me, that he was in control, but I was still scared. I think that's okay. It gave others the opportunity to minister to me. I am a person who gets things done. I like being in control of situations. Often, the easiest way to get something accomplished was to do it myself. So this situation wasn't "me." I don't like to depend on others.

After surgery and six and a half weeks of radiation treatment, I was definitely cancer-free. Wonderful words to hear. But at that point, I didn't need those words to calm me, to encourage me, to give me hope. My aunt suggested a website that would allow me to post updates and readers could post messages to me. I had found it through the words and prayers of countless people who took the time to read my updates, to encourage me, and to let me know that their prayer group was praying for me. Knowing that strengthened my trust in God. I learned to trust others more, to be vulnerable, to accept help. God is good—all the time.

Trust is not a finite thing. It grows like faith. The ability to trust is a gift from God, just like faith. Don't worry if you feel you can't trust fully. God will provide what you need to get you through.

Because He Paid for Me

CARMALITA GREEN

"For ye are bought with a price; therefore glorify God in your body, and in your spirit, which are God's."

1 Corinthians 6:20, KJV

I have this habit that I've picked up from one of my parents (my mother made me promise not to tell which parent). I like to make sure I get my money's worth out of all my purchases. I consider this to be an honorable quality; however, it does from time to time cause me to expend more energy and invest more time than the original product cost.

Recently, I found myself struggling to get the last bit of toothpaste out of the toothpaste tube. Normally this would not be a problem but this particular morning I was walking a fine line to almost being late for work. As I stood in the bathroom squeezing the life out of my toothpaste tube, I questioned myself as to why I didn't just throw that almost, basically empty tube of toothpaste away and grab the full tube in the cabinet. After all it would save much needed time. My response was, "Because I paid for it, every bit of toothpaste in that tube is mine, and it is valuable to me, and I'm not throwing it away." And in that very moment the Holy Spirit said, "Exactly."

That may seem like a strange response, but really, it's not. See, I have a hard time understanding God's unconditional love for me. It is like trying to use software for a Mac on a PC.

It just does not compute. Every time I input unconditional love into my mind, I get an error message. I often find myself having a conversation with God that goes a little like this: "God, why do you continue to allow me to live? As sinful as I am, after all the times I have asked forgiveness for a particular sin only to do it again, why do you allow me to live? Why don't you just throw me away? You must have other children who love and obey you more than I."

In order to help me understand, God uses objects and situations I do understand and know to teach me about his unconditional love. Money is something I know and understand. I understand that I do not have a lot of money. I understand how hard I have to work to earn money. I understand that money is spent faster than it is earned. And I understand that it is not only profitable but necessary to get the most out of everything that I purchase because it is mine; I not only invested money but also time in acquiring it, so I want the best from it.

The same can be said of God's longsuffering with me. God sent his only Son from the glory of heaven to earth to die the death that should have been mine. In addition to loving me unconditionally, he paid for me with the blood of his Son. I belong to him, every bit of me, and he will not throw me away. Therefore, he takes the time to mold me, yes even squeeze me into his image. Instead of throwing me away every time I mess up he will continue to work on me, scrubbing and buffing away layers of sin and filth until I am all he created me to be, until I reflect his image. It does not matter how long he has to work on me or that he will expend more time and energy than the original product cost. Because God loves me and is able to save to the uttermost, he will continue to work on me.

Why does God love me so? Because he paid for me.

Confessions of a Culinary Klutz

JAMIE SANTA CRUZ

"So whether you eat or drink or whatever you do, do all to the glory of God."

1 Corinthians 10:31, NIV

Having grown up with a mother who served up delicious, healthy, home-cooked meals as the daily fare for our family, you'd think I would have learned a thing or two about good cooking. Sadly, however, none of mom's culinary skills rubbed off on me. When I moved out on my own at 24, my competence in the kitchen was, well, nonexistent.

I still remember the first time I invited a friend over for a homemade lunch. A few days in advance, I decided on a menu—salad, potato soup, and biscuits—and called my mom for recipes. Then, shopping list in hand, I headed to the grocery store for ingredients. On the day of the lunch, I set out all my ingredients on the counter an hour before my friend was to arrive, propped up my printout of Mom's e-mailed recipes, and got to work.

It was a disaster.

"Sauté onion in oil," was step number one for the soup. I had no idea what a sautéed onion was supposed to look like. I dropped the diced onion into a pot, set it on a warm burner, then dutifully stood guard over the pot, poking it every few seconds with my long-handled wooden spoon, nervously wondering how long this sautéing process was supposed to take, anyway.

"One tablespoon fresh parsley," read the recipe. Lacking the fresh herbs, I tossed in a tablespoon of dried parsley instead. Then I noticed the equivalency directions on the side of the parsley jar: "1 teaspoon dried parsley = 1 tablespoon fresh parsley." Oops.

"Bake until lightly browned," I read in Mom's directions for the biscuits, so when I pulled the biscuits out of the oven after fourteen minutes, I agonized over whether or not my floured rounds had achieved the proper color. Gingerly lifting the biscuits off the baking sheet with a spatula, I tested one with my finger. Light and fluffy as...rawhide.

My friend was kind and said nothing about the biscuits-that-could-have-been-paperweights or the still-crunchy potatoes swimming in parsley broth.

But it was months before I worked up the nerve to invite anyone over for a meal again. For two years, any time I took a dish to a potluck, I panicked over whether or not my offering tasted "normal," and I'd nervously eye each guest as they went through the food line, painfully sensitive to whether or not someone passed over my contribution and to how much of my dish was left over at the end of the meal.

But despite my apprehension about cooking, I persisted. I pored over cookbooks, studying them for hints and tips on how to bake sandwich bread or form a pie crust. I regularly called my mom to ask about such things as how to steam broccoli or what "al dente" means. And I practiced.

Eventually, the persistence paid off. I learned how to sauté an onion and how to make fluffy biscuits. I began coming home from potlucks with bowls scraped clean, rather than with most of my contribution left untouched in the dish. And one day, after I'd finally risked inviting some friends over for soup again, I was shocked and thrilled when one guest actually asked for my recipe!

Today, being asked for recipes is no longer unusual, and I no longer feel anxious about hosting a meal. I've even developed a specialty in healthy, plant-based cooking, and my ongoing ambition in the kitchen is to see how many vegetables or whole grains I can sneak into a dish without anyone realizing they are actually eating something healthy. (Since even my husband, not a healthy eater before he married me, claims he loves my cooking, apparently my mission has been somewhat successful.)

Learning to cook—and especially learning to cook healthy meals—is no easy task.

But knowing that I am able to contribute to the long-term health of my family through nutritious cooking is definitely worth the effort. And my story goes to show that anyone—even the clueless!—can do it successfully.

Follow the Plan!

DELORES FRANCOIS

"For I know the plans I have for you …"
Jeremiah 29:11, NIV

I left my doctor's office late one afternoon in December with a mandate to lose weight.

This was not the first time the doctor had suggested I lose weight. But I had been having a hard time trying to get fully motivated to do something about it. This time she strongly suggested I lose the weight or suffer the health consequences. There was my motivation!

I set my goal. I would lose twenty pounds. Now I needed a plan. My office just happened to begin a "Biggest Loser" contest. The contest began in February and was to end in late April. I joined. I decided I would exercise, modify my diet, and drink lots and lots of water in order to achieve my goal by the end of the contest. With my plan mapped out, I was ready to put it in action!

I began briskly walking four miles each morning before I went to work. The mornings were very cold and a few mornings there was snow! In the beginning I hated getting out of my warm bed, and some days I didn't quite make it. However, I kept reminding myself of my goal and how much better I would look and feel.

I gave up the sweet stuff during the week, the snacks and soft drinks in the afternoons. I started drinking lots of water. I learned to stick to only one helping of food and smaller portions at mealtimes. As the weeks went by the weight slowly started coming off. I did have some setbacks; however, I kept my goal in mind and persevered.

I had a very good support and encouragement system in place. My brother would call me twice a week to encourage me to stick with the plan. My husband stopped filling the kitchen pantry with all the goodies we liked so that I would not be tempted. My coworkers and my girlfriends would notice and comment on how nicely I was slimming down.

On the final day of the contest, I weighed in with a loss of 18.2 pounds!

Even though I missed my goal by two pounds, I considered it a big success! I won the contest! I lost the highest percentage of weight in the contest! All my hard work had paid off! I felt physically better than I had felt in years! What a great feeling! I had followed the plan.

My action plan put me on the road to physical wellness. As a Christian, I need to have an action plan for my mental and spiritual wellness. I have set my goal. I want to be within God's will for my life and to meet him in heaven. My plan is to consistently exercise the privilege of prayer and to faithfully study God's Word. Putting the plan in action, I will reflect God's unselfish love to mankind. I will solicit the support of good Christian friends who will help me stay focused. There will be days that I will miss the mark; however, I will not give up. I will ask God for his forgiveness, grace, and mercy. People will look at me and say, "Wow, there is something special about her." They will see my spiritual beauty. Why? Because I will follow the plan!

God also had a plan. It was called the plan of redemption. It pretty much was the biggest plan the world has ever known. We are so blessed and privileged to have had a plan so beautifully and lovingly prepared for us! God's goal was to redeem fallen humanity. The plan was to send his only begotten Son, Jesus, to a sinful world. God put the plan in action at the birth of Jesus, his death at Calvary, his resurrection, and ultimately his second coming. Oh, and by the way, he sent some support and encouragement through the presence of his Holy Spirit. He could have changed his mind when he foresaw all the things that were going to happen to his precious Son. He didn't. What love! I've been redeemed because he followed the plan!

"For I know the plans I have for you ..." (Jeremiah 29:11, NIV).

The Tender Trust of Life

COLLENE KELLY

*"A righteous man regards the life of his animal;
but the tender mercies of the wicked are cruel"*

Proverbs 12:10, NKJV

The fat, translucent orange caterpillar crawled across the back patio. Spying it, my seven-year daughter triumphantly captured her prize and displayed it to one after another of the family members. Though we had hatched several butterflies over the summer, this one looked different than all the others.

We'd captured the striped Monarch caterpillars in our garden, and observed the transformational process unfold before our eyes. Each vivid green chrysalis turned nearly black before it split, and out emerged a wet-winged butterfly. The kids held the new creation carefully, the thread-like legs of the Monarch clinging to their fingers. The long, black tongue, fragile as spider's legs, uncurled, and we watched with delight as the insect drank our homemade nectar from a cotton ball.

We watched as each butterfly alternately pumped blood through their wet wings, and then rested. Soon they were able to fly, and our hearts soared with them as we released them into the summer sunshine. One of the beautiful insects' wings was crumpled, and Julie babied along "Heather," as she named her. Since she only walked, Heather spent most of her time in the cardboard box, when she wasn't being carried around. One warm day as the kids played on the porch, Heather flitted up and away, and we rejoiced she'd conquered her handicap.

But a more unusual caterpillar arrested our attention. It was late in the season, and cool weather flirted with the waning summer sun. Even if we saved the unique specimen, would there be flowers sufficient to provide for its sustenance when it hatched? We confined it in our canning jar "incubator," and after several days, a brown chrysalis replaced the caterpillar. For several months, nothing happened, and eventually I placed the jar on a shelf beside the basement steps.

In the very depths of the February freeze, Julie discovered the chrysalis open, and a new butterfly in the jar. With squeals of unequaled delight, she brought the stunning swallowtail to me. Soon it flitted across our living room, its iridescent wings catching the sunshine streaming in the window. Knowing it had no chance to survive the frigid outdoors, we boiled a new batch of nectar and soaked several fluffy cotton balls.

But despite our best efforts, this gorgeous, out-of-season insect refused our offerings. A couple days later Julie came to me, her chest heaving with sobs of a broken heart, and tears racing down her cheeks. Our butterfly was dead. I comforted her the best I could, assuring her that she had done everything possible to save the gilded insect. Julie chose a wooden box, and tenderly placed the butterfly on the scarlet lining, a lesson in life and loving, tucked in her young heart.

Life is a tender trust. We can take it, but we can't make it. It is a gift. The timeless proverb, "Teaching a child not to step on a caterpillar is as valuable to the child as it is to the caterpillar," still rings true.

Someday soon there will be new heavens and a new earth. Until then we must teach our children to respect the gift of life, whether in the person of a classmate, or in a fat, orange caterpillar crawling across the patio.

Life Is Amazing Live It Well

LINDA NORDYKE HAMBLETON

"Every good and perfect gift is from above, coming down from the Father of lights, who does not change like shifting shadows."

James 1:17, CSB

I'm happiest when I wake up breathing. I am acutely aware of the exchange of air through the lungs, the pulsating movement of blood in a vein, the billions of electric impulses that form a thought in the mind. Life is an amazing gift.

There was a time—long ago—when such things were taken for granted. Somewhere, on the edge of my memory, I can vaguely recall days when these activities took place unnoticed and unappreciated. It was a time when my body served me like a faithful assistant: It took me where I wanted to go; it did what I asked; and it communicated what I wanted to say. It was a short season when my body functioned more or less without effort—days when superficial whims and desires could nudge me to and fro. I was healthy, my soul free, my thoughts drifting like a toy boat dancing with the breeze.

And then it all evaporated like a mirage in the desert of reality. Yes, I am happiest when I wake up breathing. But today, each breath has a price; each hour costs; each day is expensive. Today the blood still pulsates, but every beat of my heart depends on a delicate balance of needles and pills.

Each day is a complex series of steps in an intricate dance to maintain life–a dance that my doctors, family, and I share together. The breathing continues, but basic bodily functions are sustained by machines, a sacrificial family, and teams of medical experts. Thoughts still form in my brain, but they are focused and strategic since clear thinking is necessary for physical survival now. And when it comes time to move, every movement is preceded by careful planning and a concerted, intentional, conscious focus of my will. A growing percentage of my day (much more than half now) is spent in bed, in pain and, at times . . . in fear.

"Life" is an amazing gift. I am more convinced of that now than ever before. But as M. Scott Peck wrote in the opening words of *The Road Less Traveled*, life is difficult.

Certainly, simple numbers cannot define us, yet the statistics that describe our lives have a story to tell. Here are a few of mine. Since contracting my disease, I have experienced:

- 128 hospitalizations
- 6.75 average days per hospitalization
- 37,500 shots
- 2 organ transplants
- 69-74 pills/day, or about 168,000 total
- 2 heart attacks
- 3 cardiac arrests
- 3 strokes
- 250 grand mal seizures and about 150 focal seizures
- 12,000 laser blasts to my eyes
- 52 inches of incisions, 255 stitches and 137 titanium staples

... And then there were the three minutes that I was clinically dead. ...

When it comes down to it, however, there is really only one statistic that matters: I have been given one more day. Just one more day. Over and over I am reminded that there are no guarantees for tomorrow—and if today is all I have, I have both the opportunity and the responsibility to embrace it, to experience it, and to invest it in something that matters.

By God's grace, when I wake up breathing, I know that I have been given one more gift, another moment of time to touch, to heal, to celebrate, and to love.

Excerpted from the book *Life Is Amazing Live It Well,* by Linda Nordyke Hambleton (Orlando, FL: AdventHealth Press, formerly Florida Hospital, 2011)

The Magic of Believing

LORRAINE JAMES-STIGGERS

"Beloved, I pray that you may prosper in all things and be in health, just as your soul prospers."

3 John 1:2, NKJV

Every day of the week, every week of the month, and every month of the year is busy and challenging for me as a wife, mother, educator, counselor, and therapist. I thank the Lord each morning he allows me to experience his miracle-working power.

One summer morning, I lay in bed trying to decide if I should get up to attend a meeting or stay in bed for just a few more minutes to rest. I remained in bed for a short while and then tried lifting my head off the pillow, my usual routine, but to my surprise I was unable to move it. After several unsuccessful attempts to lift my head, roll out, turn over or to move any part of my body, I finally realized something was seriously wrong. I lay still, looking up at the ceiling wondering, *How in the world did I get myself in this situation?* Fear swept over me as tears streamed down my face into my ears.

My husband was in another room on the other side of the house, but I was reluctant to accept the possible response he might have given so I remained still and waited. I prayed, "Lord, what should I do now? You have my undivided attention."

In a still small voice, Jesus whispered, "Have faith, I promised you that I will never leave you or forsake you. I am here. I will restore."

With those words of comfort and assurance lingering in my ears, an indescribable calm and peace embraced me and I rested in his loving arms. I was no longer angry, impatient, fearful, frustrated, and bewildered but relaxed, knowing that he was in control.

I have always been extremely active and involved in community service and ministry, participating in community outreach programs, Ingathering, church school events, walk for diabetes, drug-free marches, as a volunteer for the Red Cross, and much more. Playing tennis, bike riding, running, travelling, swimming, reading, walking, teaching, sewing, and writing have been some of my favorite pastime activities but never did I ever imagine, in my wildest dreams, that I would be unable to move when I wanted or need to move.

My husband eventually assisted me to get some much-needed help that I was more than willing to receive. I learned that my kidneys had failed. Water wasn't one of my favorite beverages. Saying "NO" when I was already overwhelmed and exhausted was difficult for me. Eating meals at the same time every day seemed virtually impossible due to my unpredictable schedule. Making sure that I got adequate amounts of rest was challenging. All of these things had contributed to my present state. And all of them had to change.

This experience led me to commit to taking better care of my health in a holistic way, encompassing the body, mind, and spirit. Even though I currently have 60 percent of kidney functioning, the Lord is keeping his promise when he told me, "I will restore."

He is doing that each and every day of my life. The Lord is continually working miracles in my life, one indicator being I am still here. He is my Restorer, my Healer, my Protector, my Comforter, my Redeemer, my Provider, my "Everything." Remember, the Lord wishes above all things that we *"prosper in all things and be in health, just as your soul prospers,"* as John wrote (3 John 1:2, NKJV).

And he wants us to believe, even when things may seem impossible: *"...for assuredly, I say to you, if you have faith as a mustard seed, you will say to this mountain 'Move from here to there,' and it will move; and nothing will be impossible for you"* (Matthew 17:20, NKJV).

On Eagles' Wings

FRANCES MORFORD

"But they that wait upon the Lord shall renew their strength; they shall mount up with wings like eagles; they shall run and not be weary; and they shall walk, and not faint."

Isaiah 40:31 KJV

Slamming the car door, I ran into the house. "Monroe has to go register the car and I'll finish packing. Is there anything I can do to help while he is gone?" I inquired.

"You can turn off the beans," my sister replied. I ran into the kitchen and immediately slipped and crashed onto my left ankle. There was a slight click and a stabbing pain. "Oh, no!" my sister cried. "I just mopped the floor and it is still wet." Strong arms gently picked me up and carried me to the front room couch.

When my husband returned four hours later, he found a tear-stained wife reclining on the couch with an ankle propped up on an ice pack. "What happened?"

he asked. I tried to explain, but sobs shook me as I realized the problem this accident was causing. He was returning to South Sudan in just a few weeks. This would drastically change plans. Monroe was only home on a short furlough and I was planning to return with him. There was no choice. He had to return. We had been spending weeks getting shots and so forth in preparation for me to return with him. Now that exciting bubbles had broken along with my ankle. Buckets of tears started flowing again.

"Let's get you to the doctor and get his advice. Then we will know how to proceed," my patient, not easily shaken husband said as he loaded me into the car. Of course, after the X-ray and all the advice, we had to change plans. I had to stay off my ankle for six weeks. He had to go back to Sudan without me again.

My broken ankle healed quickly as I waited week after week in my Lazy Boy chair, reading and praying. One night I came across Isaiah 40:31. *"But they that wait upon the Lord shall renew their strength; they shall mount up with wings like eagles; they shall run and not be weary; and they shall walk, and not faint"* (KJV). As I was pondering those words, the phone rang.

"Hello, this is the church Conference. We are making arrangements for your flight to South Sudan. Your passport and tickets should arrive within a couple of days. The itinerary is all made out for you to meet your husband. Call if you have any questions or problems." What a relief. I really had nothing to fear.

Soon, however, I was faced with decisions I had never had to handle before. Fear took over. We had travelled overseas many times, but my capable, self-confident husband had always taken care of things while I just tagged along watching the luggage. *How do I pack so I won't be overweight, get to the airport, and locate the right ticket window?* I wondered. But most of all I realized that although I could walk on my ankle again, how could I carry all my bags and make it through the terminals alone? Panic took over again. My sister reminded me that airlines offered wheelchair assistance. They would take care of me all the way. Another answer to prayer!

When the day arrived, I snapped the lock on the last tightly packed bag, picked up my purse bulging with the important passport, tickets, and other needed items. As I locked the door behind me, I bowed my head in a short prayer, then jammed the oversized baggage in the trunk of my sister's car, picked up my hand luggage, crawled into the back seat, and shut the door.

As the airplane seat belt snapped around my waist, I settled down to relax. The fear that had been gnawing inside left and I began to recall all that had happened in the last few months.

God had been so good. He had given me the opportunity to read my Bible and find Scriptures that strengthened my faith while I was recuperating. I had witnessed miracles happening almost daily. I remember reading Isaiah 41:10: *"Don't be afraid, for I am with you. Don't be discouraged, for I am your God. I will strengthen you and help you"* (NLT). Now I felt ready to spend time in our new mission field. My strength had been renewed. I could walk and I was even flying on eagle wings. What a wonderful God!

For Melinda

GLADYS JOY! BAZEMORE

"No tears are shed that God does not notice. There is no smile that He does not mark…."

Peace Above the Storm

I couldn't find a particular mobile home park, so I started knocking, to see a few more people before dark. Melinda opened her door and greeted me. She asked, "Who are you and where are you from?" I held out a flyer and said, "I'm with the Bible Story, those blue books you see in the doctor's office. Have you seen those before?" "Oh, yes," she said. "Would you like to come in and get out of this heat?" We sat down at her kitchen table, and she asked, "Haven't we met somewhere before? You just look so familiar!" She said she had the books years ago. "But my brother has them for his kids now, and I know I'll get them back for my grandchildren later," she finished. She did not want to look at big books today.

"Let me show you something really nice that we have," I said, pulling out some of our books—*My Friend Jesus* storybook, *Peace Above The Storm, God's Answers, Foods That Heal.* As Melinda glanced through *Foods That Heal,* she said, "This is good. I'm a nurse, so I'm familiar with some of this." She told me which doctor she worked for, and I said, "Oh, I've been going in there for the last twelve years to check your *Bible Story* book!"

Melinda laughed, "That's where I've seen you before. That's why you look familiar!"

When I asked if she would like to give a donation for some of the books, she gave a strong "Yes!" and went to get her checkbook.

Then she asked, "Do you have a few minutes? May I share something with you?" She left the kitchen and came back, clutching something to her heart. "I share this story whenever I can," she began. About three years earlier her husband and son-in-law had been killed in a boating accident. They had gone fishing for the day and ended up drowned. In fact, the son-in-law was lost under the water for ten days, and they had the funeral for her husband, not knowing if they would ever find the son-in-law. A year later she said she just wanted to get away for a while. So she and her two grown daughters and their little children went to their time-share vacation spot in another country.

On the very day of the anniversary of her loss, she was walking the beach alone, drawing hearts on the sand and bawling her heart out to God, grieving her dear husband of thirty years. Suddenly, a wave swept up something at her feet. She reached down to grasp it quickly. It was a piece of shell or worn coral, smoothed by waves and sand into a beautiful little heart. She stared at it in her hand, praising God through her tears that he had remembered her.

"And here it is," she finished as she handed me the frame. There was the little heart, mounted behind glass.

She told me, "I don't understand God's will, but I believe that he has used me through it all."

She started a widow's support group. As she waited for the ladies to come for the first meeting she could see her own shadow on the wall, and she thought, *How can this be? How can I be a widow? I was supposed to retire in just a few years and just enjoy life together with him.* Then she said, "Other people have told me that they have taken courage in difficulties because they say, 'If Melinda can hold up under what she's been through, we can make it through this.'"

I read to her from *Peace Above the Storm*, where it says: "No tears are shed that God does not notice. There is no smile that He does not mark…." When

I looked up, Melinda said, "I can't wait to start reading!"

We prayed together before I left, and I knew I had been sent down that road, not for a mobile home park, but for Melinda.

Safe as a Deer

LISA CLOUZET

"When I am afraid, I put my trust in you."
Psalm 56:3, NIV

"If you live here long enough, you will hit a deer" was the warning I received from more than one person after moving to rural Michigan. I had heard horror stories of deer jumping out onto the highway and causing accidents. It seemed that every other week—at certain times of the year more than others—the local paper reported on deer-versus-car incidents. I often spotted deer alone or in small herds while driving along the highway. Most of the ones I spotted were dead alongside the road. I knew that dawn and dusk were the times to be especially alert. I have to admit that I had probably become a little paranoid about driving at those times of day.

So, as I headed for the airport, I prayed for protection. "Lord, please protect the deer and me from each other!" I guided my car through the early morning darkness, fog, and snow flurries onto the highway entrance ramp. Michigan winter driving conditions added to the anxiety I felt about making my flight on time.

I had not driven more than three miles when I spotted the deer. The highway light acted as a spotlight shining down through the fog and I immediately slowed down, noting there was an exit I could use to avoid hitting the deer. Just as I was beginning to steer onto the exit ramp, the deer began moving away from my lane and off to the other side of the road.

I could hear my heart pounding in my ears as I sent up an audible "Thank you" and continued on my way.

I made my flight and arrived safely at the airport in another state where my husband was waiting for me. On the way to where we were to spend the night, I was sharing my deer encounter experience with him. A few minutes later, a large deer came running out into the five-lane freeway, heading straight for us! Miraculously, it had avoided being hit on its way to our lane and then—almost as if it were held forcibly back right at our lane— it suddenly turned on its heels and ran back across the four lanes and into the woods. I am not sure if the deer could have been more frightened than we were!

Once again, I sent up a "Thank you."

A few days later, as my husband and I drove home from our Michigan airport, I wanted to identify at which exit I had seen the deer. I figured it would be easy since the first few exits had no highway lights. Imagine my amazement when I had passed all the exits and not one had a light. I had no doubt that my prayer had been answered, but I thought I had just missed the light, so I paid special attention the next time I made the same trip. I felt goose bumps as the realization hit me—there was no mistake—there was not one light along that section of highway! Today, I am convinced that the "spotlight" came from a heavenly source rather than from a highway light.

I still live in Michigan and travel the same highways. I still have a healthy respect for the many deer that I know are out there. I still say a prayer for the Lord to protect the deer and me from each other, assured that he continues to hear and answer.

"When I am afraid, I put my trust in you" (Psalm 56:3, NIV).

Infusion

ARLENE SALIBA

"Trust in the Lord with all your heart, And lean not on your own understanding; In all your ways acknowledge him, And he shall direct your paths."

Proverbs 3:5-6, NKJV

Lost in thought as I drove to the clinic, I tried to focus my attention on the road. Yet the basic desire for food was loud and persistent. I had grabbed leftovers to eat for lunch before starting work. The hunger pangs were so strong that I gave in and ate two cold eggrolls while driving.

Finally, I exited the highway. The clinic was only a mile away. Suddenly, I became conscious to the sound of breaking glass, scraping metal, and the explosion of air on my face. Opening my eyes, I found myself in the middle of the road. Both airbags in my van had deployed and both front windows were shattered. Something was trickling down the middle of my chest: BLOOD!

What happened? Was anyone hurt? What did I hit?

A man came to my window to ask if I was hurt. I didn't think so, except for a cut on my chest. He said I had crossed the midline and hit another vehicle. It had rolled over on its side in the ditch and the driver had crawled out unhurt. The ambulance came and I was placed on a backboard with cervical spine precautions because I could not remember anything prior to the accident. All of a sudden, I was no longer hungry. In fact, I was nauseated. I protested the cervical spine precautions, but the ambulance crew thought it necessary especially with the development of nausea. They also had to consider a head injury.

After a CT scan and a few X-rays, I was released with the diagnosis of a concussion but no broken bones. What a relief!

Over the next week I would have flashbacks of my first conscious moments after the accident. I relived the sounds of breaking glass, scraping metal, and the bursting of the airbags. Sleep was fitful during those nights.

One particular night, I lay awake for a long time. The sounds played back in my head once more. The awful thought of what could have been brought fear to my heart: I could have killed or maimed the other driver. I could have been injured much more than I was. What would happen to my family if I was gone? Why didn't I make a sandwich that I could eat quickly instead of packing eggrolls, rice, and vegetables? Was there something that I could have done to prevent the accident?

In the darkness I prayed. "Forgive me, Lord, for not taking care of my body before taking care of others. This is such a bad time to have this accident. Our family cannot afford another car payment at this time. At least the van was already paid for. How is this a fulfillment of your Word in Jeremiah's writings for peace and hope? These flashbacks are not peaceful, and the pending economic burden of another car payment is far from hopeful. What lesson can I learn from this experience?"

Slowly infusing from the top of my head to the bottom of my feet came the answer. Absolute peace enveloped my being like I have never felt before. Then the message: "My child, this is not about what you have or have not done. This is not about you at all. Don't you know that the devil is after your soul? The time is not yet. This is between him and me. There is still plenty you can do for me."

Reassured that the fight was not mine, I drifted into sleep once more, never more to be disturbed by flashbacks.

A Girl's Wish, A Woman's Existence

SHAMETA WEBB

"I will praise thee; for I am fearfully and wonderfully made: marvelous are thy works; and that my soul knoweth right well."

Psalm 139:14, KJV

As a little girl, she often imagined what it would be like to be that superstar she always dreamed of being. "I could be a famous singer," she said as she stood in the mirror with her hairbrush in her hand. "I also want to be an actress and a model," she joyously imagined in her head. She believed that she could be whatever she wanted to one day.

Growing up, self-doubt and insecurities began to enter her mind as she started questioning her appearance. "Why is my nose shaped this way?" and "Why can't I be a little bit shorter, because I'm too tall?" she asked herself. She doubted her abilities to do certain things even while in the midst of others. The television and magazines only added to her insecurities at times, as she constantly saw the perfect-looking people gracing the covers and smiling as if they had everything all together.

"I know I'm beautiful, but there are just some things I would change if I could," she said. People always told her that she was pretty and she knew it also, but she just didn't always feel that way inside.

As this little girl got older and years passed by, she began to have a different outlook about herself and her life. She started to develop a closer relationship with God and the opinions of others didn't seem to matter as much anymore. She started studying God's Word and seeking his guidance and direction in her life. The closer she became with God, the more she understood the things he revealed to her. Her beauty became radiant to those she came in contact with. Her personality and presence revealed the love of God as she sought oneness with him more and more each day.

No longer did self-doubt and insecurities trouble her mind, because she became confident in the woman that God had made her to be. It was no longer about image or what she thought she should or shouldn't look like. Changing lives and helping others outweighed any of the superficial things that had seemed to matter to her before.

As a woman, God had given her that inner strength to conquer anything that came her way. Her words became so eloquent, but yet so powerful. Her beauty radiated both inside and out while captivating the attention of those that needed it the most. The love of God and the spirit of God had definitely replaced the self-doubt that had lingered in her mind as a young girl growing up.

"Women are created special by God," she said to herself, as this became apparent to her more and more. "They're so strong, but yet so fragile, taking on different roles in life. They're required to keep going because there are so many people that depend on them. In their own pain and sorrow, they have to be there to stand for others who look to them for guidance. A woman's job is never complete. God knew this beforehand, that's why he created us so special and unique."

Father, I pray for all the young girls, young ladies, and women out there who are battling with self-esteem and self-worth issues. Please touch their hearts and minds and reveal to them your love as they begin to love themselves. Let them know that no matter what they go through and experience, no matter what people say about them, they are precious to you and worth more than anyone could ever put in words.

In Jesus' name, AMEN.

CHERYL MOSELEY

"Trust in the Lord with all your heart, And lean not on your own understanding; In all your ways acknowledge him and he will direct your paths."

Proverbs 3:5-6, NKJV

As I entered the departure gate, tears rolling down my face, I turned and waved goodbye to my two best friends. Everything I owned was either packed in my suitcase, somewhere in storage, or in a container crossing the Atlantic. I was leaving my home, my country, my friends, and my family to go to a strange and lonely place. Three months before, my husband had travelled ahead of the family to the United States to begin a course of study for ministry. The only thing I was looking forward to was seeing him again.

For two years we had been praying and searching to know God's will for our lives. We felt sure that God had led us to this place, but now as I left home and friends, it seemed so hard. My security was gone; I was out of my comfort zone.

The next few months became very discouraging as all my hopes and dreams for this new adventure seemed lost. It felt like everything was going wrong and I questioned whether God really had been leading us in this direction. One thing that seemed to go wrong was selling our home. I felt sure that if this move was God's will, he would sell our home immediately without any problems. We needed to sell in order to finance the study and living expenses for the next three years. We faced many difficulties, lost thousands due to the failing economy, had buyers pull out at various stages, and eventually had to leave our country without having secured a sale.

I had great plans for my children and was determined to see them back in Christian education again. That was not to be. The differences between the schooling system of our new home and that of our own country made it very difficult for the children to continue in school. I decided to home-school my children despite having no experience in teaching whatsoever. This also meant putting my own plans aside so I could be home with my children.

Among other trials I became very discouraged with my friends back home. I had no e-mails or phone calls for weeks, maybe months after I arrived. I knew they were busy but all I needed was a friendly voice, someone interested in how I was doing, and someone who missed me. It seemed that now that I was gone they had forgotten me; at least that was what I told myself. My emotions took control and I allowed wrong thinking to dominate my life. "Why did we come here?" I kept asking myself. I felt God had deserted me.

Early on in our experience we kept coming across two verses that particularly encouraged us. They are found in Proverbs 3:5-6: *"Trust in the Lord with all your heart, And lean not on your own understanding; In all your ways acknowledge him and he will direct your paths"* (NKJV). One day, when I was feeling particularly low, my husband came home with a bunch of flowers to lift my spirits and two little cards from a Christian bookstore. One had my name written on it and the other had his name. Underneath each name was a text. My card had Proverbs 3:5 and yes, you've guessed it, his card had Proverbs 3:6!

Amazing! This was a turning point for me; it seemed God was speaking to me again. It reminded me that I had stopped leaning upon him and wasn't trusting in him. I remembered all the ways in which God had led us here. Again I turned my life over to him, realizing that the only way I was going to get through was to trust. It's the best decision I have ever made.

Trusting my life to him has bought me peace and happiness in this place. God has answered many prayers and our whole family's experience in the United States has been truly amazing. We love living here! I feel closer to God and to my family through this experience. We only have a short time left in this place, and I know my tears will be greater leaving here than they were leaving home three years ago.

I made a decision that turned my experience around. I made a choice to trust.

Exposed

NONI BETH GIBBS

"I have blotted out, as a thick cloud, your transgressions, and like a cloud, your sins; return to Me, for I have redeemed you."

Isaiah 44:22, NKJV

"Sweetie, would you please have the kids pick up the trash in the yard?" my husband asked, getting in the van to go to work. I groaned and nodded. They had been at it again, throwing stuff out the second-story window. Bottles, papers, and even a book littered the thin layer of snow. I sighed again.

"Come on kids," I called. "Dad says to pick up the trash. Hurry or you'll be late for school. And stop throwing things out the window—I don't care if it's for science or not!"

"But it's cold," they whined, almost in unison.

"Maybe so," I shot back, "but you won't like cleaning it any better when it's 40 below."

As winter had increased its hold on the chilly northland where we lived, having moved from California, I had quickly learned that the snowfall itself was not the biggest problem. The brutal winds drove the snow across the prairie, where it collected into huge drifts. The same bushes that sheltered our yard also built-up drifts, including a gigantic wave of snow along the edge of the driveway—complete with a curl on top. Pretty soon, even our drifts had drifts.

Still the naughty and short-sighted children continued to throw things out the window, trusting the snow and wind to hide the evidence. And so it did, layer upon layer, for about four months. Even a seemingly endless winter must come to an end, and at long last the trees lost their last few leaves, making way for new growth.

Temperatures rose above freezing, and the mountains of snow began to shrink. As the layers melted, the full mess of winter came into full view. It wasn't all the children. Trash had blown in from miles around, riding the swirling currents of many vicious storms before coming to rest on our property.

But though the three of them tried, there was no blaming Canada and the northerlies for the distinct piles under the upstairs windows. Pens, pencils, paper…they could almost have started a school down there.

As the snow continued to melt, every single thing they thought was so well hidden came into full view. Every secret relentlessly came to light; even the light bulbs they believed were gone forever. It took a massive effort on all our parts to get the yard cleaned up and looking decent again, and more than once I heard, "I wish we hadn't thrown this stuff all around."

So often we think we can hide the evil in our own hearts. With a thick coating of "snow" on the outside, we may appear to be just fine, even righteous. Only God knows for sure what is really underneath our protective layers—all those hidden sins that stand between us and an intimate relationship with our Creator.

When he turns the heat up, our sins are exposed. As uncomfortable as that is, he can't get rid of them till they're out in the open. And no matter how long it takes, God never runs out of patience with cleaning our hearts, time and time again.

What are you holding onto? What is keeping you from a joyous friendship with God? Let go of it. Give it to him. He has faithfully promised, *"I have blotted out, as a thick cloud, your transgressions, and like a cloud, your sins; return to Me, for I have redeemed you"* (Isaiah 44:22, NKJV).

You and I belong to him. He bought us, he forgave us, and he will cleanse us.

The Wiggly One

JANET SCHLUNT

"Do not withhold good from those who deserve it when it's in your power to help them."

Proverbs 3:27, NLT

People were gathering in the boarding area for the cross-country flight from Chicago to Portland. Southwest Airlines has open seating. I wanted to be early in line for my boarding section so I could get a choice seat near the front. That would enable me to be one of the first up the jet way. It was then I noticed the young mother with her toddler and infant. "Nobody is going to want to sit next to that wiggly boy," I thought to myself. "I'm traveling alone. I could do it. I might even be able to help the lady."

Sure enough, no one had chosen the aisle seat by the threesome. "May I sit here?" I requested. We exchanged a few pleasantries after which I suggested that she let me hold her sleeping darling while she attended to the wiggly one. Her treasure was gratefully handed over.

It was interesting to watch how the mother entertained her young son with creative drawings and tiny toys brought along for the purpose. "Are you a schoolteacher?" I asked. "Yes," she answered. "But I'm not working while my children are young." The little boy was well-behaved, but constantly moving. If she had had to hold the baby on her lap and entertain the wiggly one it would have been much more difficult. I mentally recalled some of my own journeys with wiggly ones on my lap, especially the day my own toddler cried the entire trip from Chicago to Florida, which was something of a nightmare. At least neither of these children was crying or being difficult.

The sleeping baby seemed to get heavier as time went on. The book I had planned to read remained in my bag under the seat. Sleepiness overtook me for a short while. Then we could see the snow on Mt. Hood, and I knew the flight would soon end. Finally the wiggly one slept. The mother relaxed as we commented on how it so often happens that just before landing time a child will finally drop off to sleep. The baby sister had slept all the way across the country. Now she opened her big blue eyes and smiled at me, unafraid. Then it was my turn to play little games with her.

Placing one hand over my face and not making a sound, I revealed a little bit of my face by moving one finger at a time. Then all at once my hand came away and we both smiled with delight. This was repeated several times, always with the same result. How easy it was to entertain this contented baby!

I offered to help the children into their stroller on the jetway, but the mother assured me she would wait until the plane cleared of passengers and she could manage quite well on her own.

I was still one of the early ones off the plane. In the terminal stood a young father waiting for his family to return from baby's first visit to far-away grandparents. He was easily identified from his wife's description. As I passed him, I smiled and lifted up a prayer for God's blessing on this lovely young family.

"Do not withhold good from those who deserve it when it's in your power to help them" (Proverbs 3:27, NLT).

Wake Up!

ASHLEY TARDIF

> *"My voice You shall hear in the morning, O LORD; In the morning I will direct it to You, And I will look up."*
>
> **Psalms 5:3, NKJV**

*B*eep, beep, beep-beep, beep-beep…

The imposing alarm clock brought my senses to life. In a sleepy stupor, I squinted over at the clock. How dare it say 6:30 AM! Could I really have slept the entire night? How could morning have come so quickly? Shutting my eyes against the unrecognized miracle of another day, I rested my head back on the pillow. *Just a few more minutes of peace,* I thought. *Then I will get up and running for the day. I'll merely close my eyes and relax; forget about all the demands of today. And I won't fall asleep. I won't fall asleep….*

What seemed several minutes later, I startled awake. With horror, I beheld the clock, now displaying a prominent 7:35 AM. What had I done? Oh, *why* had I fallen back asleep! Chiding myself for not heading to bed at a decent hour the night before, I threw back the blankets and hurried to dress and prepare for the day.

The indifferent altering of the clock's digits angered me while I scrambled to make myself presentable. There was so much to do, in so little time! My mind began involuntarily reciting the mental list of tasks that I needed to accomplish before the sun set that evening.

With a frown, I dashed to the kitchen for a bite of breakfast. Automatically bowing my head to thank God for my food, I realized I had neglected morning devotions–again. Guiltily, I pretended that God "understood" while I thrust into his hands my list of requests for the day.

I had thrown away the opportunity to begin my day seeking God's guidance. My 6:30 AM denial had set me up for a miserable day.

Contrast that, with this…

Feeling rested and rejuvenated from my night's rest, I awoke to the quiet of early morning. I silently slipped out of bed and down the hall to the living room sofa, where my Bible was waiting for me. Darkness dissipated as a nearby lamp illuminated the room. Reading my Bible and talking with my Father in the silence that surrounded me, I renewed my trust in him. The first rays of sunlight pierced the sky as I arose from my refuge, empowered for the daily battles ahead.

I felt prepared this time; ready for anything. Since I had spent time to pour out my heart's burdens to God, I didn't make the mistake of dumping them on others. Because I had paused to recommit myself to him, I could better trust God to help me through any obstruction in my path.

God longs to spend time with us each day. He eagerly waits for us to come to him and be filled with his presence. Of course, the devil doesn't want this to happen; he aims to keep us from God's presence in any way he can. He can't stand it when we want God's blessing more than an extra hour of sleep. He knows that those who immerse themselves in God's Word are difficult to subdue. So he fights to keep us slothful, not wanting us to recognize the power that is ours when we are filled with Jesus. The battle for time with God is a difficult one, but when we are victorious in the first battle of each day, the other battles that ensue are much easier to overcome.

By setting aside time for God each day, you are showing others who is most important in your life. And you can declare with the psalmist David: *"My voice You shall hear in the morning, O LORD; In the morning I will direct it to You, And I will look up"* (Psalm 5:3, NKJV).

Gardening 101

PATRICIA BODI

*"But grow in the grace and knowledge of our
Lord and Savior Jesus Christ.
To him be the glory, both now and to the day of eternity. Amen."*

2 Peter 3:18, NASB

In early June, after a cold Michigan spring, my apartment complex gave me an offer I couldn't refuse—a free garden space. Being a "city girl," my only gardening experience was roses and tomatoes in pots on my patio and flowers around the perimeter of my condo. I didn't even bother to read how to plant a garden. I just went and purchased plants at a greenhouse. Even at that I failed, since I wouldn't listen when my friend told me I was getting enough tomatoes for the entire church! I went ahead and bought what I thought was a flat of 12 tomato plants which turned out to be 42! The mosquitoes were so bad that I just grabbed a few plants, paid for them, and took them home.

Now it was time to get them into the ground. I looked around the house for whatever I could find to dig some holes in which to put my precious tomato plants. I used a handy little kitchen gadget–don't laugh–it worked.

Now the serious part of gardening–watering! We were told to use the water from a nearby creek, but no one cut a path down there so that was impossible. I had to resort to lugging gallons of water from the outdoor spigot at the closest apartment building. It didn't help that I had plenty of company lugging water. I mean, does any of them have herniated discs, L3-4, L4-5 and Klippel-Feil syndrome in their cervical spine, carpal tunnel in both their wrists, and not even one good knee?!

I decided I couldn't afford forty-two tomato cages, so I again improvised–dowel rods at 29 cents each. As I looked at my finished garden space and compared it to others, I couldn't help being embarrassed at my rudimentary attempts. Other garden spaces appeared very geometric, sort of like they used a yardstick. Their plants were in a straight line! Some had built up mounds, had mulch and straw and lattice-type frames for their plants to climb. I was outclassed before I got started.

I learned from my neighboring plots, by observing what my fellow gardeners did, and talking to them. I did some mulching, too, and learned that weeding was a worse job than the watering, and like watering, it had to be done every day, too. My garden was beginning to look positively beautiful to me, anyhow. I got some compliments from my neighbors. Now I couldn't straighten up my rows but was relieved when someone observed that my rows were perfect diagonally! Maybe I was ready for prime-time gardening.

Then the woodchucks came and feasted on our gardens while we slept. I still don't know how to get rid of them!

What lessons did I learn from gardening? I took pride in the fact that because of me, these plants were actually growing. When I used a little introspection, I realized my life kind of paralleled my gardening attempt. While I had no clear plan when I started, I learned as I went along, borrowed, and adopted ideas from others. If it weren't for other individuals in my life, I never would have made as significant a contribution as I had made. And the Master Gardener kept on watering and weeding even when I seemed distant and unapproachable. He was watching me grow.

What happened next surprised even me. After I got my garden looking good, I'd found myself weeding the garden spaces on either side of mine when the owners didn't do it. After all, the weeds might "jump" over into my space, I told myself. Isn't that a lot like my life—always trying to help others even when they don't ask or maybe even care? What are those fancy buzz words?—*co-dependent, enabler*? Yeah, gardening is a lot like life.

How does your garden look? Are your plants in nice straight rows? Are you weeding other's spaces? Is the Lord watering and weeding even when you are careless and nonchalant about your Christian experience?

Waiting for God

LYLAN SHEPHERD FITZGERALD

"Wait patiently for the LORD. Be brave and courageous. Yes, wait patiently for the Lord."

Psalm 27:14, NLT

The morning air was fresh and crisp as I sat in the rocking chair on the lodge porch at the women's retreat. Fog hovered over the valley the same way sadness and grief lingered over my heart. The loss of my loving husband to cancer still consumed me, even after three years. Friends reminded me that I must get on with my life—but "get on" to where? I felt lost and very alone.

My prayers had focused on a home, the one John and I had planned to build before his illness. Just a log cabin on our farm, but a place of my own, my first true home. Not a rental house or either of our parents' homes, but my own. Once again I poured out my heart to my heavenly Father, and then sat quietly waiting. The psalmist's admonitions to "wait patiently upon the Lord" must have been written for me. It can be uncomfortable to sit in his presence, just waiting. But practice has taught me that this is the time when my faith, courage, and strength are renewed.

Never have I been disappointed when I spend time with him. This morning was no exception. His presence filled the air around me, and his voice reached into my heart. "I will give you a home for hurting hearts—a place of healing."

My spirit lifted like the fog in the valley. Sharing the promise with my special church "sistas" and friends doubled my joy.

Before his death, John and I had discussed developing a portion of the farm into a small subdivision and selling the lots to friends so we could finance our log cabin. Now I felt confident that this was the right decision and could hardly wait to see what God would do. Plans took shape quickly and amazing people stepped forward to help. An engineer friend offered to design the subdivision and help submit plans to the authorities. A contractor who came to talk about a gate became the perfect choice to install the road and utilities. Another friend helped design the entrance and a huge entry gate. A woman I had worked with years ago attended church with a builder who specializes in log homes.

Everything fell into place and moved quickly; then disaster struck. Land prices fell, and no one was able to purchase the lots at the established prices. The historical significance of the property was questioned, resulting in months of delays in construction. The county's use of a small strip of adjoining property had changed, making potential buyers uneasy about security.

Property tax appraisals had to be appealed. And, all the while, the interest on the bank loan continued to grow.

How could this happen? The development had been dedicated to God—for his glory! How could he allow things to get so out of control? Wait! Is he in control—or have I taken over? I suddenly realized that I had been too busy to spend time with my Friend. How could I not see that I had strayed from his plan? Much time has been spent asking for his forgiveness and then waiting, waiting, waiting for him.

I could almost hear him sadly whisper, "Girlie, you're just getting too big for your britches."

Now we are back to the original plan—his plan. Keep it simple. Make it affordable for the people who need to be here. Trust him to provide for my needs. I'm still not sure when or how my home will be built. But one thing is certain—I must step out in faith, trusting him. I must allow my faith to grow by spending time with him—as I would any true friend.

Sit in his presence—perhaps even climb up onto his lap and rest my head on his chest. What divine peace and security! It's all the home I could ever hope for.

Walk On

LAURA BRADFORD

> *"He will wipe every tear from their eyes, and there will be no more death or sorrow or crying or pain. All these things are gone forever."*
>
> **Revelation 21:4, NLT**

The autumn day was dark, with clouds hanging heavily over our valley and dry wind pummeling everything in its path. I sat indoors, monitoring the skies every few minutes, longing for fair weather so I could take my daily walk. Sun and exercise seemed as if they'd be the perfect remedies for my aching body and melancholic mood.

The responsibilities of handling Dad's funeral had left me tense and exhausted. As I wrote out checks to the mortuary, the florist, and the cemetery, I was flooded with memories of my own husband's passing only four years earlier. Here I was again, laboring alone over the ugly details of death. It took what little strength I had to hold onto Jesus. But I refused to weep since I knew my loved ones' souls were safe. About an hour before sunset, I determined I'd take a walk regardless of the dark, blustery conditions. Since I had the funeral bills to mail, I planned to walk only a few blocks to our local post office, then return home.

As I fought against the wind, I felt as though my legs were carrying the heaviness of my heart. But the busy atmosphere at the post office brought some welcome relief.

Just seeing people and saying hellos helped to lift my mood. After mailing the bills, I started toward home but sensed the Lord prompting me, "Go further–along your regular route."

I groaned.

Normally, I'd walk a three-mile circular route, up a hill and down again. But my usual energies were gone, especially with the wind fighting me every step of the way. After taking a few minutes to stare longingly in the direction of home, I turned around and surrendered my will to the Spirit's guidance.

Trudging away from the post office, I started up the hill along a quiet lane. But it was too quiet. The silence, the gray skies, and the effort of climbing all combined to overwhelm me. Long-overdue tears began rolling down my cheeks. Afraid someone might see me, I said, "Lord, why did you ask me to walk farther? You knew it would be too much. Can't I just go home?"

"But I have a gift for you," I sensed him telling me.

That aroused my curiosity! I dried my eyes and forced my limp legs to make the steep climb to the halfway point of my usual walking route.

As I rounded a corner, I saw my gift! Low-hanging clouds were departing, leaving a band of blue just above the western horizon. Within seconds, the setting sun dipped down to peek at me from under the clouds. Warm rays kissed my face, while rose-colored light streamed across the mountainsides and down our long valley. They were like beams of hope penetrating my gloom and reviving my strength. I quickened my pace as I walked on, thanking God profusely for this perfect gift.

Just as I'd turned west to face the brightness, a car pulled up beside me. To my surprise, my best friend hopped out. "Mind if I walk with you for a few blocks?" she asked. "I don't want to miss the sunshine."

"Come on," I invited. "This is great!"

She ended up walking me all the way home as we "oohed" and "aahed" over a landscape bathed in shifting rays of pink and golden light. Her friendship, coupled with the glorious evening, turned my focus forward, to a joyous time when we'll all be together, with no more tears … forever.

God knew just what I needed to lift my lonely, grieving heart–a reminder of eternal hope and the company of a good friend.

Bonded by Wounds

MONICA AMES

> *"Surely he took up our pain and bore our suffering,
> yet we considered him punished by God, stricken by him, and afflicted.
> But he was pierced for our transgressions, he was crushed for our
> iniquities; the punishment that brought us peace was on him,
> and by his wounds we are healed."*
>
> **Isaiah 53:4-5, NIV**

One bright spring morning when I was just sixteen years old, I grabbed my ten-speed bike and rode over to my friend Carly's house for a visit. Carly and I liked to sit at the small table in the corner of her dad's kitchen and sip peppermint tea from fancy cups, imagining that we were grown up ladies at some fashionable café in Paris.

We chatted the morning away as the sun rose higher in the sky. What started out as typical teenage girl talk soon took a sharp turn and drifted into more serious topics. I knew it had not been easy for Carly since her Mom had left, but I had no idea what she was going through.

Carly started opening up and sharing things that normally she had kept hidden inside. Soon I was also sharing deep hurts that were close to my heart. Before long we were both in tears. I leaned over and wrapped my arm around Carly's shoulders and then we hugged each other while we cried. Amidst our sobs we heard a noise at the window. It was her faithful golden retriever, Jack, looking at us with big dark questioning eyes, wondering what was the matter. "Just look at us! We're a mess," Carly exclaimed.

Then we sat back blinking away the tears and burst into laughter together. The rest of the morning consisted of more laughter and tears. As I rode home later that day breathing in the fresh spring air, life seemed different somehow. The problems I faced were just the same but my outlook had changed. I now had a friend who understood and cared. It was a healing relationship for both Carly and me. Because of that time we shared I was able to help Carly get to know the Bible and Jesus Christ. I gave her several texts to consider, but as time went by she moved and we lost contact.

Years later when I was in college I received an unexpected call at about 3 AM. There was a small timid voice on the other end of the line. It was Carly. We were about 700 miles apart and it had been quite some time since we had spoken, but I quickly woke up with excitement in just hearing her voice again.

Carly told me that her life had become unbearable and I was the only person she wanted to talk to. She was in a dangerous relationship that she needed to get out of. It thrilled my heart to hear that Carly had saved all the Scriptures that we had gone over together and she still treasured them. I was able to encourage and pray with her so she could take a stand for what was right. Then I sent her the prettiest, most uplifting card I could find.

I'm so glad Jesus brought Carly into my life. The love and caring of our friends can go a long way in lifting our spirits. Being a friend to someone brightens our own days, but the friendship we can share with Jesus is infinitely greater than what we can experience with any other person. Just as Carly and I were able to share our hurts, so Jesus has borne all the weight of sin upon himself and longs to share that message with us. Of course, Christ wants to hear our hurts and pains, and has a deeper empathy than any human being could ever provide. He is there for us in the darkness of every night and the wee hours of every morning. He understands our feelings even more than we can understand them ourselves. He's waiting at our kitchen table, or any other place we might happen to be, for us to pour out our hearts and share our joys with him.

Why not give him a try?

One of My Favorite Gifts

LISA CLOUZET

"In everything I did, I showed you that by this kind of hard work we must help the weak, remembering the words the Lord Jesus himself said: 'It is more blessed to give than to receive.'"

Acts 20:35, NIV

Christmas can be such a joyful time, a time when love is shared from one heart to another. It can also be a very lonely time. It was the beginning of a Christmas season, while doing chaplaincy visitation in an assisted care facility, when I met Marva—an amazing woman who was struggling with the holiday blues. She had suffered a stroke which left her partially paralyzed on her right side. Her children were about my age and busy with their own lives. Not wanting to add to their burdens, she had chosen to live in a small room which she had furnished with the bare necessities and a picture or two. Marva's life at that point was routine and uneventful, except for the occasional visit from a family member or friend.

That December day, I asked Marva what she enjoyed most about Christmas. She seemed to gain energy as she recalled Christmases past and all the traditional festivities which she had enjoyed around her family. Her eyes glistened as she described exploring the neighborhood's Christmas lights and decorations. She reminisced as though she would never again experience that pleasure. Before I had really thought about it–about how busy I was, about how many Christmas preparation items I had on my list, about how little time I had to get ready–I was inviting Marva to go on an outing to explore the Christmas lights! She was surprised and excited and accepted my offer.

The day came for our outing. It had been a long day and I felt low in energy as I dragged myself to the assisted care center. I was energized when I saw Marva, all dressed up and waiting to go on her adventure. Her eyes sparkled, her face glowed, and she chattered like a schoolgirl. For Marva, ordinary tasks took more time than usual. We donned her coat, ambled to my minivan, and then the fun began. We pulled and tugged and managed to get her up into the van and settled into her seat and seatbelt. After stowing her walker in the back seat, we were off!

We had gone less than a mile when Marva mentioned she was warm and would like to remove her coat. Normally that would not be a big deal.

But removing her coat involved pulling over, wrestling her out of her jacket and back into her seatbelt. Marva and I laughed uncontrollably at the thought of what a show we were providing for passersby. It also provided good medicine for us!

The excitement of the evening grew as we passed by house after house decorated in bright lights and seasonal fare. After an hour of exploring, Marva was satisfied and ready to return to the place she called home. Knowing she seldom had the opportunity to leave the center, I asked her if there was anything else she would like to do while we were out. Her eyes lit up once again as she said she would love to stop somewhere and buy her favorite candy bar. Since she was allowed sweets in her diet, I pulled over at the next gas station. When I returned with two of her prized candy bars, she delightedly opened one and slowly ate it on the way back.

Marva shared with me the gift of appreciating people and relationships, and of treasuring the important moments in life. By responding to her love and her simple request, both of our lives were enriched and another memory made. She seized the moment and so did I.

Marva did not live to see another Christmas, as she passed away the following spring. I think of her as each holiday season rolls around. I try to look for gifts to share that money cannot buy. I also look for the extraordinary gifts in ordinary moments.

"In everything I did, I showed you that by this kind of hard work we must help the weak, remembering the words the Lord Jesus himself said: 'It is more blessed to give than to receive' " (Acts 20:35, NIV).

About the Authors

Sara Alsup has been teaching Bible studies for many years and speaks regularly as part of a spiritual retreat ministry.

Monica Ames was the VBS director at her church and also served as a member of a women's ministry board at the time of her writing.

Carla Baker serves as director of women's ministries in Silver Spring, Maryland. She previously lived near Fort Worth, Texas, where for eleven years she also served as director of women's ministries.

In 1996, **Gladys Joy! Bazemore** became a full-time literature evangelist in Georgia. At the time of her writing, she lived and worked in Oklahoma.

Patricia Bodi was active in women's ministries in Michigan at the time of her writing. Her passion is walking so she enjoys leading women in "Walking with Jesus" at retreats.

Jean Boonstra is Associate Speaker for the *Voice of Prophecy*, and Executive Producer for *Discovery Mountain*. Jean is committed to encouraging women to serve God in the role that He has called them to. She and her husband Shawn live in Colorado and are the proud parents to two adult daughters.

Laura L. Bradford's writings have been published in several inspirational anthologies compiled by *Guideposts*, *Chicken Soup for the Soul,* and *A Cup of Comfort*.

Dawn S. Brown and her family live in Orlando and are committed to living the CREATION Life principles.

Dorothy L. Brown served as a registered nurse for about thirty years, with most of her experience in mental health.

Alicia Bruxvoort describes herself as "a lover of Jesus Christ, a seeker of abundant life, and a freelance writer and speaker." She blogs daily at *www.AliciaBruxvoort.net*.

Tami Cinquemani is the WholeLife Church Pastor of Worship & Liturgy. She believes Micah 6:8 gives clear and concise direction for life: "to act justly, love mercy, and walk humbly with God."

Lisa Clouzet serves as a chaplain and licensed counselor. She currently teaches in Berrien Springs, Michigan.

Julie Cook traveled around the world to finally settle down in Florida, where she teaches writing and speech at AdventHealth University.

Joanne Cortes and her husband serve in pastoral ministry. She says that her main desire is to be a reflection of Jesus and share his love.

Terri Cruze is a nurse by trade and is the author of two books, *Finding Peace in the Midst of Chaos* and *Joy for the Troubled Heart*.

Dorothy Davis is a retired elementary school teacher. At the time of her writing, she served as a mentor for a Christian school in Gary, Indiana.

Robyn Edgerton oversees the branding and development of CREATION Life as director of Mission Strategy at AdventHealth and is committed to helping people live whole-person healthy.

Tricia Smith Edris is the Chief Consumer Officer and Senior Vice President for AdventHealth. With over thirty years of experience, Tricia leads AdventHealth's consumer initiatives and provides executive oversight for consumer research, innovation, experience, and digital strategy.

Lizbeth Fernandez is the mother of a beautiful girl who has Down Syndrome. She makes her home in Orlando.

Lylan Shepherd Fitzgerald is a Licensed Massage Therapist who enjoys writing. She is active in women's ministries.

Ana Boudet Forman has taught religion to middle school students for more than twenty years. She enjoys reading, "deep, change the world" conversations, and Florida Gators football.

Delores Francois volunteered at a local community crisis organization as a helpline counselor and a rape response advocate at the time of her writing.

Noni Beth Gibbs has written two books, *Malchus: Touched by Jesus*, and *Peter: Fisher of Men*. She lives in Montana with her husband, Jack, and their three adventuresome children.

Jenni Glass works as a logistics manager at Adventist Health in Roseville, California.

About the Authors

Carmalita Green is a Registered Dietitian for the Alabama Department of Public Health.

Linda Nordyke Hambleton is the author of *Life Is Amazing Live It Well*.

Lisa Harper is a popular speaker and author of over a dozen books including *A Perfect Mess* and *Stumbling Into Grace*. Her style combines sound scriptural exposition with easy-to-relate-to anecdotes and comedic wit. Visit her at www.LisaHarper.net.

Helen Heavirland taught a writing class at the time of her writing and has published more than 200 short pieces. Her latest book, *My Enemy, My Brother*, is a true story out of World War II which gives rise to hope.

Codi Jahn enjoys spending time with friends and family, traveling, and delicious food. At the time of her writing, she volunteered at a local high school where she coached the varsity volleyball team.

Sharon Jallad is married and has two grown children. She is a Director and Chief Operating Officer of Accredited Surety and Casualty Company, Inc.

Lorraine James-Stiggers is an author, poet, avid reader, and motivational speaker who has traveled across America and abroad conducting workshops and seminars for churches, schools, and businesses.

Collene Kelly has written for the Indiana Conference Family Life Department, the *Adventist Review*, and the NAD Women's Ministry Department.

Mary Kendall made her home in Columbia, Missouri where she enjoyed writing and serving as a dental hygienist at the time of her writing.

Jaclyn King teaches college and high school English. The written word is a passion for her. She loves cooking and sharing healthy, wholesome meals with family and friends. Her son Julian is the light of her life.

Patty Knittel enjoys writing, golf, reading, travel, and her cats. Her writing has appeared in various Christian magazines.

Betty Kossick is the author of *Beyond the Locked Door* and *Heart Ballads*. She has also served as a contributor to fourteen other books.

Stephanie Lind serves as Executive Director of Population Health at AdventHealth Central Florida. She is a daughter, sister, aunt, wife, and mother of 2—all who encourage her to live life to the fullest!

Amanda Maggard serves as the President and CEO of AdventHealth Zephyrhills and AdventHealth Dade City. She and her husband, Michael, have been married for 16 years. They have two sons, Griffin and Landry.

Omayra Mansfield, MD MHA FACEP is an emergency medicine physician and Chief Medical Officer. She is wife to Frederick, and mother to Elizabeth and Alexander. They are her constant reminder to be grateful for all the little joys in life.

Tracey Mastrapa has experienced God's transformative power and has witnessed miracles both grand and small. She is a work in progress, and God is patiently molding her as He prepares her for both earthly and eternal tomorrows.

Cynthia Mercer is a registered nurse and enjoys serving in full-time ministry along with her husband.

Frances Morford spent over thirty-five years serving in Africa with her husband. Her ministry work included teaching English and the Bible as well as typing, home economics, and health classes.

Cheryl Moseley lived in Berrien Springs, Michigan with her husband Andy and their children at the time of her writing. She homeschooled her children and studied psychology while there.

Mulenga Mundende makes her home in Kansas where she writes and serves as a certified registered nurse anesthetist.

Judith Newton wrote a column for her local newspaper from a spiritual perspective at the time of her writing. She also hosted a weekly radio spot on her church's Christian radio station.

Carla Gober Park, PhD is the Executive Director of Faith Community Strategy in Mission and Ministry at AdventHealth corporate office and the Assistant to the President at AdventHealth University.

Sperantza Adriana Pasos is an author and inspirational speaker whose greatest treasure is her family. Her passion is sharing the eternal hope in her amazing God with all she meets. *Hopeinpresentdanger.com.*

ABOUT THE AUTHORS

Alicia Patterson is an Assistant Religion Professor at AdventHealth University. Her favorite places are around the table with her family, in nature with friends and family, and in the Word with God.

Kimberly Quinnie has created Bible studies for the deaf and hard of hearing. At the time of her writing, she resided in South Korea, where she was a missionary English instructor and Bible teacher.

Eve Rusk makes her home in Boise, Idaho. She enjoys working with children's programs at her church.

Arlene Saliba currently teaches in the nursing program at Andrews University and works part-time as a family nurse practitioner.

Jamie Santa Cruz is a freelance writer and editor in the Denver area.

Janet Schlunt has served as a departmental secretary at a Michigan university and a secretary in the office of the president at Pacific Union College.

Ashley Tardif lives and writes in the great state of Maine. Her life's dream is to be a full-time missionary in Eastern Africa.

Jean Thomason has released numerous books, videos, and CDs for preschoolers. An accomplished singer, songwriter, and performer, Jean communicates biblical truth through her character named Miss Patty Cake. For more, visit *www.MissPattyCake.com*.

Stacey Tol has an MFA in creative writing. She likes to play games with her hilarious family, bake sweets, climb rock walls, travel to new places, and listen to audiobooks while she's cleaning.

Diane Thurber serves as president of Christian Record Services in Lincoln, Nebraska.

Pam (Lister) Tucker, a Canadian artist, lives in Texas with her husband Mike. A full-time music minister and writer, Pam is helping plant a church with Mike in Dallas, Texas when not traveling.

Shameta Webb writes from Orlando, Florida where she has lived and worked in healthcare for the over a decade.

SCRIPTURE REFERENCES:

Unless otherwise indicated, all Scripture quotations are taken from the Holy Bible, New Living Translation, copyright 1996, 2004, 2015. Used by permission of Tyndale House Foundation. Used by permission of Tyndale House Publishers, a Division of Tyndale House Ministries, Carol Stream Illinois 60188. All rights reserved.

Scripture quotations marked NIV are taken from the Holy Bible, New International Version,® NIV®. Copyright © 1973, 1978, 1984 by Biblica, Inc. ™

Scripture quotations marked (NirV) taken from the Holy Bible, New International Reader's Version ®, NirV Copyright © 1995, 1996, 1998, 2014 by Biblica, Inc.® Used by permission of Zondervan. All rights reserved worldwide.

Scripture quotations marked (RSV) are taken from the Holy Bible, copyright © 1946, 1952, and 1971 National Council of the Churches of Christ. Used by permission. All rights reserved worldwide.

Scripture quotations marked (ESV) are from the Holy Bible (English Standard Version®), copyright © 2001 by Crossway, a publishing ministry of Good News Publishers.

Scripture quotations marked (CEV) are from the Contemporary English Version Copyright © 1991, 1992, 1995 by American Bible Society. Used by permission.

Scripture quotations marked (GNT) are from the Good News Translation (Today's English Version, Second Edition) Copyright © 1992 American Bible Society. Used by permission.

Scripture quotations marked KJV are taken from the Holy Bible, The King James Version.

Scripture quotations marked NKJV are taken from the Holy Bible, The New King James Version. Copyright © 1982 by Thomas Nelson, Inc. Used by permission. All rights reserved.

Scripture quotations marked MSG are taken from *The Message*, copyright © 1993, 2002, 2018 by Eugene H. Peterson. Used by permission of NAVPress. All rights reserved. Represented by Tyndale House Publishers, a Division of Tyndale House Ministries.

Complete Jewish Bible (CJB) © 1998 by Messianic Jewish Publishers and Resources. Used by permission.

All Scriptures quoted from The Revised Geneva Translation of the Holy Bible (RGT) is used by permission of its publisher, Five Talents Audio. More information about this transaction can be found at https://www.5talentsaudio.com/rgt.

Scripture taken from the Common English Bible®, (CEB) Copyright © 2010, 2011 by Common English Bible. Used by permission. All rights reserved worldwide.

Register this new book:

Visit AdventHealthPress.com

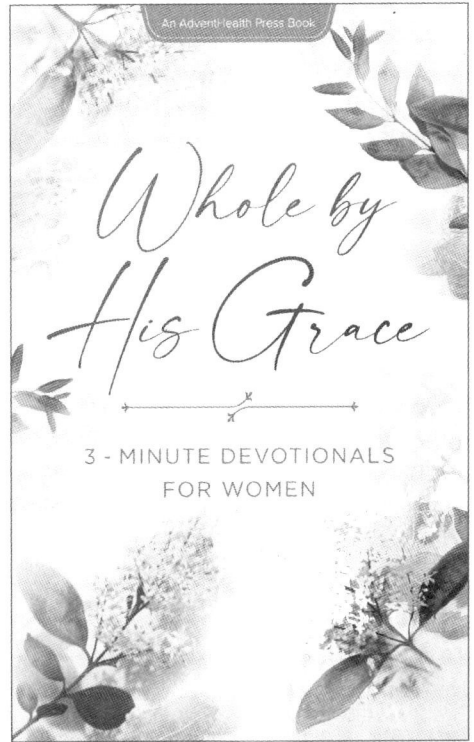

BENEFITS OF REGISTERING:

FREE replacement of lost or damaged book

FREE audiobook – *CREATION Life Discovery*

FREE information about new titles and **giveaways**

ABOUT THE PUBLISHER

AdventHealth is a connected network of care that promotes hope and healing through individualized care that touches the body, mind and spirit to help you feel whole. Our hospitals and care sites across the country are united by one mission: Extending the Healing Ministry of Christ. This faith-based mission guides our skilled and compassionate caregivers to provide expert care that leads the nation in quality, safety, and patient satisfaction.

Over 5 million people visit AdventHealth each year at our award-winning hospitals, physician practices, outpatient clinics, skilled nursing facilities, home health agencies and hospice centers to experience wholistic care for any stage of life and health.

AdventHealth Press publishes content rooted in wholistic health principles to help you feel whole through a variety of physical, emotional, and spiritual wellness resources.

To learn more visit AdventHealthPress.com.

RECOGNITIONS

CLINICAL EXCELLENCE. AdventHealth hospital campuses have been recognized in the top five percent of hospitals in the nation for clinical excellence by Healthgrades. We believe that spiritual and emotional care, along with high-quality clinical care, combine to create the best outcome for our patients.

TOP SAFETY RATINGS. We care for you like we would care for our own loved ones — with compassion and a priority of safety. AdventHealth's hospitals have received grade "A" safety ratings from The Leapfrog Group, the only national rating agency that evaluates how well hospitals protect patients from medical errors, infections, accidents, and injuries.

SPECIALIZED CARE. For over ten years, AdventHealth hospitals have been recognized by U.S. News & World Report as "One of America's Best Hospitals" for clinical specialties such as: Cardiology and Heart Surgery, Orthopedics, Neurology and Neuroscience, Urology, Gynecology, Gastroenterology and GI Surgery, Diabetes and Endocrinology, Pulmonology, Nephrology, and Geriatrics.

AWARD-WINNING TEAM CULTURE. Becker's Hospital Review has recognized AdventHealth as a Top Place to Work in Healthcare based on diversity, team engagement and professional growth. AdventHealth has also been awarded for fostering an engaged workforce, meaning our teams are equipped and empowered in their work as they provide skilled and compassionate care.

WIRED FOR THE FUTURE. The American Hospital Association recognized AdventHealth as a "Most Wired" health system for using the latest technology and innovations to provide cutting-edge, connected care.

PARTNERSHIPS

WALT DISNEY WORLD. AdventHealth has partnered with the Walt Disney World® Resort for over 25 years. As the Official Medical Provider for runDisney and Official Athletic Training Team of ESPN Wide World of Sports, AdventHealth has played a critical role in enhancing the Disney Parks and Resort operations and experiences for athletes.

In 2011, AdventHealth and Disney opened the Walt Disney Pavilion at AdventHealth for Children, which is now one of the premier children's hospitals in the nation, setting standards for innovation, quality and comprehensive care. The child-centric healing environment is designed to keep kids comfortable is complemented by a staff of world-class doctors, specialists, nurses and healthcare professionals utilizing advanced technologies, therapies and treatments. AdventHealth also collaborated with Disney to create AdventHealth Celebration, a cutting-edge comprehensive health facility that was named the "Hospital of the Future" by the Wall Street Journal.

STRATEGIC SPORTS. AdventHealth's commitment to whole-athlete care and innovative care models extends throughout our strategic sports partnerships, which span across multiple professional sports leagues including NBA, NFL, NHL, and NASCAR. AdventHealth is the Official Health Care Provider of the Orlando Magic, Lakeland Magic, Orlando Solar Bears, and Sebring International Raceway, Exclusive Hospital of the Tampa Bay Buccaneers, Official Health and Wellness Partner of the Tampa Bay Lightning, as well as the Official Health Care Partner and a Founding Partner of the iconic Daytona International Speedway.

In addition, through our 20+ year partnership with Florida Citrus Sports, AdventHealth has provided comprehensive health care services to collegiate athletes as the Official Health Care Provider for the Cheez-It Bowl and Vrbo Citrus Bowl.

ADDITIONAL RESOURCES

The Hidden Power of Relentless Stewardship
Dr. Jernigan shows how an organization's culture can be molded to create high performance at every level, fulfilling mission and vision, while wisely utilizing - or stewarding - the limited resources of time, money, and energy.

Leadership in the Crucible of Work

What is the first and most important work of a leader? (The answer may surprise you.) In *Leadership in the Crucible of Work*, noted speaker, poet, and college president Dr. Sandy Shugart takes readers on an unforgettable journey to the heart of what it means to become an authentic leader.

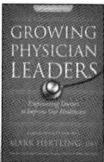

Growing Physician Leaders
Retired Army Lieutenant General Mark Hertling applies his four decades of military leadership to the work of healthcare, resulting in a profoundly constructive and practical book with the power to reshape and re-energize any healthcare organization in America today.

The Love Fight

Are you going to fight for love or against each other? The authors illustrate how this common encounter can create a mutually satisfying relationship. Their expertise will walk you through the scrimmage between those who want to accomplish and those who want to relate.

Scalpel Moments
A scalpel moment can be one of painful awareness, disturbing clarity, sorrowful regret. It can also be a moment of positive awakening that can reveal, restore, and renew. Ordained minister Dr. Reaves highlights stories about life's difficult or revealing moments that remove layers of confusion, bitterness, or fear and restore one's trust in God.

Whole By His Grace

Whole by His Grace was written by women sharing the real struggles, triumphs, and lessons they have learned to inspire you with hope and courage as you face each day. Start each day with a story of hope or finish your day with a sense of His wholeness.

AdventHealthPress.com

ADDITIONAL RESOURCES

Life Is Amazing Live It Well
At its heart, Linda's captivating account chronicles the struggle to reconcile her three dreams of experiencing life as a "normal woman" with the tough realities of her medical condition. Her journey is punctuated with insights that are at times humorous, painful, provocative, and life-affirming.

Forgive To Live

In *Forgive To Live: How Forgiveness Can Save Your Life,* Dr. Tibbits presents the scientifically proven steps for forgiveness — taken from the first clinical study of its kind conducted by Stanford University and Florida Hospital.

Forgive To Live Devotional
In his powerful new devotional Dr. Dick Tibbits reveals the secret to forgiveness. This compassionate devotional is a stirring look at the true meaning of forgiveness. Each of the 56 spiritual insights includes motivational Scripture, an inspirational prayer, and two thought-provoking questions. The insights are designed to encourage your journey as you begin to *Forgive to Live.*

Simply Healthy: The Art of Eating Well – Diabetes Edition

Simple, enticing, delectable, the recipes in *Simply Healthy: The Art of Eating Well – Diabetes Edition* will convince even the most skeptical that your food can taste good AND be good for you!

Eat Plants, Feel Whole
For over thirty years, Dr. Guthrie has been helping his patients gain better health through an evidence-based, whole-food, plant-based lifestyle. Now, in *Eat Plants, Feel Whole,* he shares not only his years of expertise with you, but the scientific evidence to back it up as well.

Eat Plants Feel Whole Journal

Everything you need to succeed with the *18-day Eat Plants Feel Whole* Plan. The companion journal is an important and welcome addition to the field of healthy nutrition and lifestyle medicine.

AdventHealthPress.com

LIVE LIFE TO THE FULLEST

CREATION Life is a faith-based wellness plan for those who want to live healthier and happier lives and share this unique, whole-person health philosophy. By consistently practicing the principles of CREATION Life, we fulfill God's original plan for our lives, which is to live and be happy!

Our mission is to help you live life to the fullest, but we don't stop there. Feeling great is a feeling worth sharing, and we have the tools and resources to equip you for a health ministry.

Visit us at **CREATIONLife.com**
to get started on your journey to feeling whole!